The World of Turner

TIME
LIFE
BOOKS ®

Other Publications:

THE GOOD COOK

THE SEAFARERS

THE ENCYCLOPEDIA OF COLLECTIBLES

THE GREAT CITIES

WORLD WAR II

HOME REPAIR AND IMPROVEMENT

THE WORLD'S WILD PLACES

THE TIME-LIFE LIBRARY OF BOATING

HUMAN BEHAVIOR

THE ART OF SEWING

THE OLD WEST

THE EMERGENCE OF MAN

THE AMERICAN WILDERNESS

THE TIME-LIFE ENCYCLOPEDIA OF GARDENING

LIFE LIBRARY OF PHOTOGRAPHY

THIS FABULOUS CENTURY

FOODS OF THE WORLD

TIME-LIFE LIBRARY OF AMERICA

GREAT AGES OF MAN

LIFE SCIENCE LIBRARY

THE LIFE HISTORY OF THE UNITED STATES

TIME READING PROGRAM

LIFE NATURE LIBRARY

LIFE WORLD LIBRARY

FAMILY LIBRARY:

HOW THINGS WORK IN YOUR HOME

THE TIME-LIFE BOOK OF THE FAMILY CAR

THE TIME-LIFE FAMILY LEGAL GUIDE

THE TIME-LIFE BOOK OF FAMILY FINANCE

TIME-LIFE LIBRARY OF ART

The World of Turner

1775-1851

by Diana Hirsh
and
the Editors of TIME-LIFE BOOKS

TIME-LIFE BOOKS, Alexandria, Virginia

About the Author

Diana Hirsh began her writing career as a journalist specializing in public affairs, and has worked for several national magazines in Washington and New York. In pursuit of her long-standing interest in art, she has done graduate study at the New York University Institute of Fine Arts. Her particular interest in Turner started with the purchase of two of his watercolors. Formerly Associate Editor of the TIME-LIFE Library of Art, Miss Hirsh is presently Senior Text Editor of TIME-LIFE Books.

The Consulting Editor

H. W. Janson is Professor of Fine Arts at New York University. Among his numerous publications are History of Art and The Sculpture of Donatello.

The Consultant for This Book

John W. McCoubrey, Professor of the History of Art at the University of Pennsylvania. is author of American Tradition in Painting and editor of American Art, 1700-1960 in Sources and Documents in the History of Art.

On the Slipcase

A tower of flames fills the night sky over the Thames and the burning Houses of Parliament in this detail from Turner's monumental evocation of a famous London catastrophe. (For the entire painting see pages 154-155.)

End Papers

Front: Turner's economical yet satisfyingly complete pencil sketch, made about 1809, shows the city of London from a height in Greenwich Park.
Back: Seen through the trees, where a herd of deer rests, is Petworth, the estate of Turner's friend and patron Lord Egremont, and the scene of many of the artist's happiest days.

CORRESPONDENTS: Elisabeth Kraemer (Bonn); Margot Hapgood, Dorothy Bacon, Lesley Coleman (London); Susan Jonas, Lucy T. Voulgaris (New York); Maria Vincenza Aloisi, Josephine du Brusle (Paris); Ann Natanson (Rome). Valuable assistance was also provided by Carolyn T. Chubet, Miriam Hsia (New York).

Contents

I

An Eccentric
in the Establishment

The old man's request was a strange one. Aboard the steamboat *Ariel*, out of Harwich, preparations were afoot for a bad storm that was brewing. The passenger was persistent. Others might want to go below; he wanted to be lashed to a spar on deck. He was a little man, almost gnome-like, and plainly battered by time. But his sharp gray eyes were impelling, and the crew, in the English tradition of tolerance of eccentricity, complied with his wish. Tied to his perilous post for four hours, Joseph Mallord William Turner, England's leading painter, absorbed and observed the onslaught of the elements.

Turner was not much given to talk, and people only learned of his exploit through the medium in which he expressed himself best. When the Royal Academy opened its annual exhibition in London in May of 1842—just after his 67th birthday—he displayed his *Snowstorm* with a terse note about the experience on which it was based. The painting exudes power: the awesome power of the forces that inspired it, the slashing power of the hand that fashioned it. The ship is barely discernible in the savage swirl around it, yet the viewer feels himself on board, not watching the storm but enduring it.

As with many of Turner's unruly evocations of nature's moods, this work is better appreciated today than it was in its own era. His contemporaries perceived his gifts, but tended to be uneasy when he exercised them to the fullest. At such times he seemed too wild, too careless of established canons of art. The reviewer who damned *Snowstorm* as "soapsuds and whitewash" spoke for most of his colleagues. Turner's retort was spirited. "What would they have?" he asked his champion, John Ruskin. "I wonder what they think the sea's like? I wish they'd been in it!" In a calmer moment he recalled: "I did not expect to escape, but I felt bound to record it if I did."

The dedication implicit in these words helps explain, in part, the homage Turner has begun to receive more than a century after his death. The seascapes and landscapes on which his greatness rests represent a branch of art that has long since become outmoded. But whatever the subject matter—or lack of it—the modern artist believes above all in the need for commitment. Theme and style matter less than the actual experience of painting itself; the sensations that incite and accompany it matter as much as the visible result. Many decades before this esthetic was articulated Turner understood and acted upon it.

In other fundamental respects, too, today's artists find a kindred spirit in Turner. Living in an age in which classic formulas of painting still prevailed, he used or ignored them at will. Many of his works follow traditional rules of clarity, balance, mass and perspective. But in his greatest achievements Turner abandoned these precepts, intuitively pursuing paths that were to become major highways to modern art. He saw color for its own resplendent sake rather than as a means of describing objects. He saw light as a radiant entity rather than as a vehicle of dramatic effect. Often he made a shambles of form, dissolving recognizable realities in a haze of indistinctness or drowning them in a torrent of abstraction.

"Pictures of nothing, and very like," the essayist William Hazlitt labeled such Turnerian efforts. Many thought Turner mad. Others denounced what they saw on his canvases as blots and blotches of vulgar colors laid on as if with a trowel instead of a brush. To 20th Century painters this litany sounds an all-too-familiar refrain. It only confirms their view of Turner as an artist miraculously ahead of his time.

Both professionally and personally, Turner was a man of boundless complexity. For all his radical departures in art, he was no rebel, no framer of manifestos. All through his long career he dwelt contentedly, if sometimes controversially, within the bower of England's artistic Establishment. But he had an eye to his future place in the annals of art: he was addressing posterity when he bequeathed some 300 paintings, 300 watercolors and 19,000 drawings to the nation, on condition that they be housed in a separate exhibition hall to be known as Turner's Gallery (a condition that was never met). His aim was not to feed a swollen ego but to offer a comprehensive look at the evolution of his works. "What is the good of them but all together?" he asked.

His enormous output—the Turner Bequest included only those pictures he had kept for himself or did not sell—affirms the futility of any attempt to place him in a mold. Certainly he could not have amassed his vast oeuvre had he conformed to the popular fancy that expects a great artist to agonize over every brush stroke. Turner was fast and fluent. An innate sureness of hand, combined with a firm habit of industry, propelled him through six prolific decades. The wonder is not that some of his efforts were mediocre but that so many were first-rate.

Turner further confounded the popular image of the artist by being decidedly provident. As businesslike in selling as in producing his art, he piled up a fortune of some £140,000, worth almost three million dollars in today's terms; much of it came from the publication of engravings based on drawings he made for the purpose. Associates joked about his penny-pinching. He astonished them by willing the bulk of his wealth to the establishment of a fund for needy English artists—a magnanimity thwarted in the courts by his relatives.

A thoroughgoing pragmatist, Turner never struck poses about his art. The one mystery he encouraged concerned the filmy mixtures he used to achieve his incomparable atmospheric effects. About his technique itself he was matter-of-fact, if not very specific. Early in Turner's career an older painter, Joseph Farington, asked him how he went about his watercolors, then his main pursuit. The reply would have fitted his later oils as well. Farington noted in his diary: "Turner has no settled process but drives the colours about till he has expressed the idea in his mind."

Turner could be just as casual toward philosophizings on art. The story is told that he was present when some esthetes engaged in an evening of pompous talk about principles. He listened in silence, then finally rose to go. "Rummy thing, painting," he grunted, and walked out.

The intricacies of Turner's personal life could have inspired a Freudian field-day. He lived it on three separate levels, seldom connected. There was the social Turner, who relished the gala affairs of the Royal Academy and visited the estates of patron friends, fishing and bird-shooting and making himself agreeable to the children and the ladies. On such occasions he could be quite charming in a gruff, awkward way; he may have fallen short of the suave gallant, but neither was he the boor that hostile opinion held him to be.

There was also the filial Turner, whose lower-class roots were a far remove from the elegance he savored on his social rounds. His father was a barber; his mother's forebears were butchers. She died, insane, when Turner was in his twenties, and for the next 25 years Turner and his father were uncommonly close. After the senior Turner retired and until his death when his son was 54, "Daddy" and "Billy" shared houses both in London and in the country nearby. Gracious living and open-handed hospitality were well within Turner's means, but the two men subsisted modestly, even shabbily, and preferably in seclusion. Their affinity included a marked physical resemblance: both were keen-eyed, beak-nosed and unusually short. In the Turners' singularly tender relationship the son fretted over the father's well-being and the father lent an eager hand with studio chores. What thoughts he harbored about his son's works are unrecorded. Turner once remarked, fondly, that "Daddy never praised me for anything but saving ha'pennies."

Of the third life Turner lived much is suspected and little is proven. He never married—his paintings, he sometimes said, were his children. He lacked the looks to which women lost their hearts; he was so conscious of his unprepossessing self that as a youth he hesitated to paint his own portrait lest potential patrons conclude that such a man was incapable of beauty in art. Yet Turner had strong sexual appetites. Even if no other evidence existed there is indication enough in the drawings of nudes and of lovers in embrace that appear here and there in his sketchbooks. Other such drawings were unearthed by John Ruskin in a posthumous inspection of his idol's legacy. In a burst of Victorian piety, and thinking to protect Turner's good name, he burned them.

Ruskin, later to become the grand panjandrum of English art criticism, was 44 years Turner's junior and knew him only in his last decade. Nevertheless, he may have been privy to some information that

Turner's less intimate friends could only surmise. The inference is drawn from a curious letter Ruskin wrote in which he listed seven "main characteristics" of Turner that would provide "the keys to the secret of all he said and did." Among them were irritability and obstinacy ("extreme"), uprightness, generosity, tenderness of heart ("extreme") and infidelity, by which Ruskin meant Turner's lack of religious faith. The seventh trait was sensuality, and of this facet of his subject's character Ruskin admonished, "Don't try to mask the dark side."

The letter was written in 1858, seven years after Turner's death, as a guideline for a London journalist, Walter Thornbury, who planned a biography of Turner. To Ruskin's discomfiture, Thornbury, whose previous literary efforts had run to such tomes as *Turkish Life and Character*, produced an opus that fixed a sensational imprint of Turner on the public mind. It was a picture of a man who, behind a front of respectability and undoubted artistic genius, was a sot, a womanizer, a begetter of bastards and, in his old age, a habitué of low sailors' haunts. These revelations moved the *Quarterly Review* of April 1862 to compare Thornbury to a Parisian *chiffonier* (ragpicker) who, basket in hand, goes about gathering "every bit of filth and tinsel that comes in his way." But the image of the artist orgiastically "wallowing in Wapping" —then, as now, one of London's grimier districts—became so entrenched that it lingers to this day.

What may be accurately deduced of Turner's "dark side" depends on evidence less lurid, partly the testimony of his friends. Some recalled a lad seen around Turner's studio who was assumed to be his natural son because of their striking likeness. Others recalled occasions at the Royal Academy when the normally unkempt Turner arrived in natty dress—such as a red-velvet waistcoat—suggesting a woman's touch. A more solid tidbit was served up in Farington's diary. Since Farington was so meticulous a memoirist that he even recorded the seating plans of dinner parties he attended, there is no reason to doubt an entry about Turner that he made in 1809. It reads: "A Mrs. Danby, widow of a Musician, now lives with him. She has some children."

Shorn of embroidery, the central facts of the enigma of the private Turner appear to be that he had two liaisons of some duration. The first, in his early maturity, was with Sarah Danby, by whom he is believed to have had two daughters and a son. The second, from some time in his late fifties on, was with another widow, Sophia Caroline Booth, who presided over a Chelsea hideaway Turner inhabited from time to time under an assumed name. He did drink heavily later in his life, but this seems to have been at least partially induced by a dental problem: ill-fitting teeth made it hard for him to eat solid food. As for his "wallowing in Wapping," it turns out that he had good reason to go there: to collect the rents on some property left him by a maternal uncle, including a pub called *The Ship and Bladebone*.

Viewed from the 20th Century, Turner's peccadilloes seem less remarkable than the passion for privacy that led him to conceal them so carefully. For the prudish Victorianism that was set agog by Thornbury's purple passages had just barely begun to emerge when Turner died in

1851. During most of his 75 years the world of Turner was a lusty one in which—from royalty on down—anything went, and in which the measure of a man was not his morals but his mettle.

Between 1750 and 1850 England became the richest and most powerful nation on earth. It was a time of immense vitality of thought and deed, a time in which Englishmen created and invented, conquered and explored. If there were occasional large troubles, in the form of fractious Yankees or a strutting Napoleon, there were large yields as well. The loss of the American colonies was offset by a strengthened hold on Canada, and the gain of most of India and all of Australia. Two decades of costly war with France resulted in Napoleon's rout and the further expansion of empire. Trade expanded too, fueled by an Industrial Revolution at home whose blessings were mixed, but whose machine-made bounty was incalculable.

In exchange for the new urban industrialism, England forfeited its old rustic innocence. The yeoman who farmed his own freeholding and the weaver whose cottage was his workshop gave way to a less self-reliant symbol of the lower classes: the factory hand in a slum town. Social conscience was slow to awaken to his exploited state, and now and then he agitated and rioted. What he sought, however, was the reform of specific abuses rather than the wrecking of established order. Even in his plight he shared in the prevalent sense of national solidarity.

For those with talent and drive, the supposed rigidity of the English class structure proved more theoretical than real. A Turner who began his life over a humble barbershop could end it in an honored crypt at St. Paul's Cathedral. A miner's boy, George Stephenson, could teach himself to read at 18 and go on to build the world's first successful steam locomotive. The operator of a hand-loom could borrow to buy a few power-looms and rise to be a textile magnate; his sons might intermarry with the daughters of the country gentry.

Neither the gentry nor the loftiest aristocrats wholly deserved Voltaire's gibe at them in his aphorism of the English nation—"froth at the top, dregs at bottom, but the middle excellent." Upper-class life had its substance as well as froth, its concerned liberals as well as callous diehards, its scholars as well as rakes. Around the turn of the 19th Century English society was, in the words of the historian G. M. Trevelyan, "as literary and cultivated as it was fashionable, athletic, dissipated and political. . . . It had faults, of which drunkenness and gambling were the worst, but it lived a life more completely and finely human than any perhaps that has been lived by a whole class since the days of the free-men of Athens."

One great bond united Englishmen of every level: an enormous pride of country. The same poor wretches who knew they would be hanged for picking a pocket of more than twelvepence could patriotically mob a foreigner in London whose dress they deemed too alien. The same village craftsmen whom the factory system had stripped of a livelihood could cheer the laurel-wreathed coaches that sped through the countryside with the news of victory at Waterloo.

It was this national pride that helped make English art, for a period of about a hundred years, pre-eminent in the Western world. The two signal achievements of that art, portraiture and landscape, directly reflected England's love affair with itself; in them the nation held a mirror to itself and found itself good. Portraits acclaimed the wellborn and wealthy, the stylish and gifted. Landscapes idealized England's every corner. In oil, watercolor, pen and pencil, artists echoed Shakespeare's paean to his country: *This other Eden, demi-paradise . . . This precious stone set in the silver sea . . . This blessed plot, this earth, this realm, this England.*

For England's painters, the onset of its golden age in art was a heady time. It meant the end, at last, of two centuries of dominance by foreigners. Through the late Tudor and Stuart eras and into the reign of the House of Hanover, native-born artists had seen the plushest portrait commissions go to Europeans who had settled profitably in London: first a German, Hans Holbein, then a Fleming, Anthony van Dyck, a Dutchman, Peter—born Pieter—Lely, and, most recently, another German, Godfrey—born Gottfried—Kneller. Although portraiture had been an English strength since the miniaturists of Queen Elizabeth's time, the polished products of Continental hands had more cachet. Kneller's popularity was such that he reportedly managed, with the aid of an army of assistants, as many as 14 sitters in a day.

English painters also found other injustices to rail at. When one of their wealthy countrymen decided to buy a work of art he was likely to choose an Old Master—real or fancied—from Italy, Holland or France. When he decided to enlist an artist's services to decorate a sumptuous new home he was also likely to look abroad; the lively Venetian muralists and ceiling-painters were in special demand. English artists felt consigned to second-class status, forced to take the leavings of commissions or to assume a helper's role, anonymously painting the draperies or lace or hands in portraits by the stellar few.

Increasingly they fought back. Their chauvinist outcries led Treasury officials to threaten to bar payment for a ceiling painting in the Queen's Bed Chamber at Hampton Court if the commission went, as planned, to the Venetian Sebastiano Ricci; it was awarded instead to a man of sound Dorset stock, James Thornhill. Another famed Venetian suffered subtler treatment. Antonio Canaletto's sparkling views of Venice were prized souvenirs for Englishmen visiting that city on the Grand Tour. Encouraged to go to London to fatten his fortune, Canaletto was met with a whispering campaign that labeled him an impostor and reduced him to advertising for customers.

A campaign was also aimed at shaming the English collector out of his Continental bias. Theater audiences roared at a comedy called *Taste*, in which a peddler of fake foreign masterpieces happily gulled a Lord Dupe, a Sir Positive Bubble and a Sir Tawdry Trifle. The "picture jobbers" got a blistering in an article in the *London Magazine* in 1737. It was they, the author charged, who gave the English a name as easy marks and also belittled every work by an English hand. Their motive, he said, was sheer greed—to profit on imported shiploads of "dead Christs, Holy Families, Madonnas and other dismal dark subjects."

Fittingly, the man who fired this salvo was Thornhill's son-in-law, William Hogarth, who has gone down in history as the first great painter of unmistakably English stamp. While turning out his biting pictorial satires on manners and mores and his forthright portraits—"phizmongering," he called this—Hogarth also labored in the broader cause. It was plain that neither he nor his contemporaries would get very far without an effective showcase for their efforts. Few collectors came to their studios and fewer invited them to their homes; in England at the time there were neither galleries nor museums, and native offerings would hardly have been welcome if there had been.

Hogarth hit upon a scheme: he and his colleagues would offer some of their works to be displayed on public view at London's new Foundling Hospital, which had been built through the philanthropy of a sea captain who was one of Hogarth's patrons. A less likely repository of art was hard to imagine. On the gates hung a basket for the receipt of unwanted infants, and when the strain on facilities grew too great, crowds of women outside drew lots to determine the entry or rejection of their babes in arms. Hogarth's plan caught on nonetheless; hundreds of visitors, plain and fashionable, picked their way through milling mothers and squalling children to inspect the first collection of English art ever assembled in open exhibit.

Hogarth's venture taught connoisseurs a lesson in the merits of home-grown talent, and artists a lesson in the merits of group action. In the next two decades several societies of painters formed, flourished briefly, and faded. Then, in 1768, the Royal Academy of Arts came into being. From the start it enjoyed the favor and financial support of the monarch, George III, and all the prestige his patronage conferred. English art had come a long way since the stage character of Lord Dupe, when shown a painting described as the work of a living Englishman, airily declared, "Oh! then I would not give it houseroom."

By the time of the Royal Academy's emergence Hogarth was dead. It fell to another painter to transform England's pleased acceptance of its art into unabashed ardor. Joshua Reynolds' credentials made him a splendid link between the old days and the new. He was born and bred in Devon, yet trained in Italy and properly reverent of the heritage of Europe. The portraits in which he specialized were at times penetrating, at times feats of silken flattery. As remarkable as his skill was his self-esteem. His soon-celebrated "Grand Style" of painting applied also to his mode of life. Unlike earlier artists, Reynolds would not let himself be treated as a tradesman. His chosen habitat was the company of the illustrious. "As His Majesty said to me last night" was a phrase that came easily to him. It was inevitable that he should be knighted, and elected the Academy's first president—an eminence he was to occupy pontifically for 32 years.

Reynolds' towering rival was Thomas Gainsborough. The son of a Suffolk cloth merchant, Gainsborough had scant use for the upper crust. Gentlemen, he once observed, "have but one part worth looking at, and that is their Purse; their Hearts are seldom near enough the right place to get a sight of it." While he lacked Reynolds' grandness he was clearly his match in painting. Gainsborough's portraits were softer, his approach less cerebral; whoever the sitter, the result was a kind of poetic beauty. The rich and the famous flocked to patronize the one painter or the other, and sometimes both. Together Reynolds and Gainsborough gave English portraiture its unique flavor and its lasting appeal.

At the peak of his career Gainsborough bared a heretic thought in a letter to a friend. "I'm sick of Portraits," he wrote, "and wish very much to take my viol-da-gamba and walk off to some sweet village where I can paint landskips and enjoy the fag-end of life in quietness and ease." Gainsborough's yearning to devote himself to landscapes was a feeling other artists shared. As yet only a few had indulged it, but in time landscape painting came to preoccupy the second half of England's great era in art as portraiture had the first.

The passion for landscape that engulfed the English—artists and non-artists alike—was a phenomenon a later age finds puzzling. To many modern viewers landscape painting seems the quaintest and least interesting of all the traditional varieties of art; the quick wizardry of the camera has dispelled the need for other records of remembered vistas. But the sameness some see in the landscape works of yesterday lies only in the eye of the beholder. Landscape art afforded its practitioners wide scope. It could be factual, idealized, romantic, fantastic; soothing or frightening; a show of virtuoso accuracy or a vehicle of deep-felt emotion. At its finest it posed the basic question of man's relation to nature and its Creator. An awareness of this was often movingly voiced by a remarkable painter who, with Turner, was to enrich English landscape painting as Reynolds and Gainsborough enriched English portraiture: John Constable. In a letter to his wife Constable once wrote: "Everything seems full of blossom of some kind and at every step I take, and on whatever object I turn my eyes, that sublime expression of the Scriptures, 'I am the resurrection and the life,' seems as if uttered near me."

The earliest English landscapists felt a certain diffidence. Formidable exemplars existed. In the 17th Century men of other nations had perfected the art, and seemingly they had said it all. There were the Frenchmen Poussin and Claude, the former's landscapes austere and ordered, the latter's gently idyllic. There were the Dutchmen Rembrandt and Ruisdael, Hobbema and Cuyp, who ranged superbly from the romantic to the realistic in their depictions of Holland's quiet countryside. Some of Europe's landscape masters, like its portraitists, moved to England to tap the opportunities there. Among them were the marine painters Willem van de Velde and his son, both of whom had unblushingly switched sides in the running Anglo-Dutch naval warfare of the late 17th Century, and had turned out battle scenes that trumpeted England's victories as once they had the homeland's. The younger Willem's more tranquil seapieces set still another example to emulate.

England's landscape artists were never to deny their debt to the Continent, but as self-assurance grew, their art took on a character of its own. First, however, they had to convince potential patrons that landscape paintings by native hands were worth the purchase. When buying art, the English could be as practical as when trading woolens and chinaware. As a rule, a man who commissioned a work frankly expected it to proclaim his station in life. Once his own and his family's features were preserved in paint, he was likely to want the same for his country house or—in the case of the hard-riding, sport-loving squire—for his horses and dogs.

Artists amiably served these conceits, and proved the value of their work to a newly interested public. George Lambert pioneered in views of houses; George Stubbs popularized the sporting picture, celebrating the racehorses and fox hunts of the gentry; George Morland produced scenes of rural life and happy villagers. In theory these works were distinct from pure landscape painting, yet in them meadows and thickets and lakes were almost always to be seen. Sometimes nature claimed attention only subliminally; gradually, however, it encroached on more and more of the pictorial space.

Gainsborough, too, waged psychological war on landscape's behalf. By his own account the kind of composition he preferred used human figures merely "to create a little business for the Eye to be drawn from the Trees in order to return to them with more glee." A patron's reaction was probably not glee when a projected family group turned out to be as much a landscape painting as a portrait. Still, such so-called "open-air conversation pieces," as well as Gainsborough's "fancy pictures" of rustics in Arcadian settings, prepared the way for works in which landscape took over entirely, uncluttered by human life.

In many Gainsborough works the landscape is patently contrived. But at its best, his vision of nature appears as if seen through the sweetest of dreams. The woods are darkly inviting, the foliage blurred. To one brother Academician, however, Gainsborough's landscapes looked like so much "fried parsley." The author of this thrust, Richard Wilson, was one of history's most irascible artists, and one of its cheekiest: he thought nothing of dabbing India ink on a rival canvas at an Academy exhibition in order to darken tones lighter than his. In kinder moods he gave Gainsborough a grudging sort of due, but his own concept of landscape was very different. Wilson had spent a fruitful period in Italy in the 1750s, then swarming with foreign artists devoted to the memories of Poussin or Claude or Rembrandt. Wilson's comrades in Rome were ever prowling the countryside in search of a particular kind of vista, one with a "picturesque" quality. A ruined Roman aqueduct framed by cypress trees might possess this quality—in short, a view that instantly called to mind a picture demanding to be painted.

The picturesque beguiled Wilson, as did the marvelously luminous atmosphere of Italy, and he began painting light-bathed landscapes in an ordered, serenely classical style. When he returned home he abandoned an undistinguished career in portraiture in favor of landscapes pure and simple—majestically simple. The human element appeared only unobtrusively. Concentrating on the play of light and dark on massed forms, Wilson endowed the natural beauties of England and of his native Wales with a grandeur never before perceived. His contemporaries, however, saw little enough to praise; Wilson died poor and obscure, unaware that in time he would be hailed as England's first serious challenge to the landscape supremacy of the French and Dutch.

By the turn of the century, and the early manhood of Turner and Constable, the situation had changed. An English school of landscape painting was well underway, its worth unquestioned and its practitioners numerous. Patrons no longer had to be persuaded; the goal now was excellence and the realization of a more personal kind of expression. The masters were still respected—Turner eagerly hunted for Wilson's birthplace in a Welsh valley, and Constable saw Gainsborough in "every hedge and hollow tree" in the East Anglian fields where each had roamed as a boy. But the two young artists were to chart their own courses.

Both painted freely and inventively, increasingly heedless of old restraints. Their differences were large. Constable sought simple truth; Turner mixed reality with imagination. Constable's colors sparkled, Turner's blazed. This latter distinction was underscored by Constable himself in a remark in their later years. Before the opening of an Academy exhibition in which they were to be represented side by side, Constable was touching up his canvas with vermilion when Turner walked in. He surveyed the scene, wordlessly daubed a bit of flaming scarlet on his own work, a seapiece hitherto dominated by grays, and departed. With a few quick strokes he had weakened Constable's effect, and Constable knew it. A friend came by inquiringly as he stood bemused. "Turner's been in and fired a gun," he said.

The comment was rueful, but not bitter. Though they were never to be close friends, the two men respected each other. Of the two, Constable could be infinitely more gracious, and, unlike the tight-lipped Turner, he was generous in his compliments. He once asked a friend: "Did you ever see a picture by Turner, and not wish to possess it?"

Turner was, indeed, the most spectacular of all of England's landscape painters. Yet a magnificent irony attaches to his art. While he could and did excel at the kind of recognizable vista that stirred his compatriots' pride, his greatest landscapes no more belong to England than to any other country. Turner took as his text the essential elements of nature—air, light, earth, water, wind, fire—and in his brilliant compounding of them produced views that are every man's. Today in England tourists are offered an excursion to "Constable Country," redolent of the landscapes of that master. No tour is, or could be, offered of "Turner Country," for as envisioned in his more memorable works it transcends all national boundaries.

Such an eloquent artistic achievement stands in curious contrast to Turner's own beginnings. He was city bred; except for a stay with an uncle in the country when he was 10, he spent his youth in the clamor and jostle of London. He was born there in Maiden Lane, behind Covent Garden, on April 23, 1775. It was St. George's Day, honoring England's dragon-proof patron, a day thought to be of good omen. But little in Turner's childhood suggested fortune's favor. Home was a few dingy rooms above his father's barbershop. Family life was shattered by a series of violent scenes by his mother, who was gradually going mad —a misery deepened by the death of a daughter, the Turners' only other offspring.

Outside the house things were more agreeably distracting. Maiden

Lane was, as Thornbury put it, "a mere dim defile between houses clothed with the smoke of centuries." Like most London streets in that day, it was clogged with mud, litter and slops tossed from windows. Still, its narrow confines breathed vigor. There was always the din of vendors' cries, a stream of hackneys and sedan chairs, of gentlemen on horse and strollers on foot. One attraction was the shopwindow of the engraver J. R. Smith, whose mezzotints were spreading the fame of Reynolds' portraits. At No. 21, across from where Turner lived, was the Cider Cellar, where men supped on deviled kidneys and stout, sang raucously and talked Whig and Tory politics.

Around the corner was the vast square of Covent Garden, with its fruit and vegetable and flower stalls, its wooden hustings from which Parliamentary hopefuls declaimed, and its church, St. Paul's, by the architect Inigo Jones, where the Turners had been married and their son baptized. Hard by were the Covent Garden and the Drury Lane theaters, and the taverns and coffeehouses that were the Bohemia of London's wit and talent. A world more suited to Billy Turner's interest was a few minutes' jog away at the riverside. The Thames, Ruskin later rhapsodized, was to prove dearer to the boy than "Lucerne lake or Venetian lagoon," and its ships, "that mysterious forest below London Bridge," a finer tonic than "wood of pine or grove of myrtle."

The interlude at his uncle's in outlying Brentford, a change perhaps dictated by his sister's fatal illness, gave the young Turner his first whiffs of sootless air, and most of his formal schooling. Legend asserts that on the walls of the Brentford Free School he made chalk drawings of hens and cocks, and that the view from its classroom inspired his first sketches of birds and trees. A better proof of his budding ambition is an ink-and-wash copy of an engraved view of Oxford, signed and dated "W. Turner, 1787." A self-assured effort for a 12-year-old, it was followed by other drawings, also based on published engravings but often embellished with original touches. Besides talent, shrewdness was already at work; he earned tuppence from a Brentford resident for each plate he colored in a volume of picturesque English views. Back in London again, he moved on to occasional work with architects' renderings, on which he washed in the blue skies.

Proudly, Turner's father hung the boy's drawings—on sale at two or three shillings apiece—around the barbershop. As a gateway to a glorious career in art it was unorthodox but astonishingly direct. The shop's proximity to Covent Garden's fashionable haunts brought in customers of substance. The period was one of the many in which the plumage of the English male outdid the female's. Buckled shoes, fitted breeches and a fancy-buttoned coat of brocade had to be topped by an elegantly powdered wig. The wig's dressing and styling were the barber's functions, and while Turner clients pondered a choice of wig modes ranging from "the staircase" to "the pigeon's wing" they had time to look around. One, a clergyman, so admired the drawings of the barber's boy that he mentioned them to an Academician friend. Shortly, Turner, at age 14, was granted a probationary term in the Royal Academy school; he completed it in a few months and was approved as a full student. A

At the Royal Academy Turner often displayed not only his paintings, but also himself in the throes of creating them. The Academy allowed artists a few so-called "Varnishing Days" for putting finishing touches on their canvases before each show. But in this brief time Turner often totally transformed a work, and gave colleagues who crowded around a lively artistic performance as he did so. Turner, pictured here by S. W. Parrott, cut a funny figure with his paunch and his beaver hat, stooping, twisting and flicking brush and palette knife across the canvas. He would work intently for hours, then suddenly snap shut his paintbox and dart from the gallery. "There, that's masterly," observed another artist. "He does not stop to look at his work; he *knows* it is done, and he is off."

year later, in 1790, his *Archbishop's Palace, Lambeth*, a proficient watercolor, went on display at the Academy's annual exhibition. It was the first of 57 such exhibitions in which his works were to appear.

The pace of weightier events during Turner's first 15 years was extraordinary. Paul Revere made his ride the week Turner was born; Parisians stormed the Bastille as he prepared for the Academy school. In England over the same period Watt built his first commercial steam engines, Crompton his spinning mule, Cartwright his power loom. Prosperity was high. While intellectuals mulled the implications of the revolutions in America and France and the quieter one at home, the haves—titled, landed and mercantile—pursued pleasures riotous and genteel. Some did adopt a more sober tone of enterprise to fit the new industrialism, but in general the old easy morality prevailed. London, with almost three quarters of a million people, was a capital of exquisite refinements and gaudy dissipations.

Over all brooded George III. Seen as a vile tyrant by his erstwhile American subjects, at home he was irreverently dubbed "Farmer George." However others might disport, plain living was his choice. He liked to drop in on cottagers and chat about crops; an evening at home, with the mother of his 15 children, would include backgammon, with lemonade and perhaps a muffin, which he enjoyed toasting himself. He was diligent in his duties but not noticeably endowed with intellect; he was, indeed, disturbingly inclined to ramble.

In 1788, in his 28th year on the throne, he became deranged; one of the acts that placed the court on alert was his insistence on shaking hands with the branch of a tree at Windsor in the belief that it was the King of Prussia. Strict confinement followed for almost a year. The doctors' polite diagnoses of "flying gout" and "phrenzy fever" fooled no one. Gossip from the royal chambers reported, in full detail, that George was howling like a dog or getting under a sofa to converse with his Savior. Then, in early 1789, he recovered. The acerbic Horace Walpole noted: "The King has returned, not to his sense, but to his nonsense."

George also returned to grappling with the annoyance of his oldest son, whom he loathed. The Prince of Wales, pink-cheeked and plumply handsome, was now 27 and had already packed in the experience of other men's lifetimes. He was enormously in debt, partly as result of an extravagant household and a true connoisseurship of art, partly through immoderate gaming and wenching. But the Prince had also committed a larger folly. In 1785 he had secretly married Maria Fitzherbert, twice a widow, who was not only a commoner, but, much worse in an age when Popery was a bugaboo, a devout Catholic as well. The marriage was never openly acknowledged, although the relationship continued on and off for 25 years, and it was never officially dissolved; it was the subject of endless gossip throughout England and the cause of acute anguish to George III. But Maria's allure was impressive: 40 years later, after a disastrous dynastic marriage and a succession of mistresses, her royal lover would go to his grave with her picture in a locket around his neck.

The King's period of derangement in 1788 had offered the Prince hope for a way out of his troubles. If he became Regent because of his father's incapacity to rule, he would not only be rid of the old man's constant criticism but he would also control the royal purse strings. Encouraged by his cronies in Parliament, he had even arranged for a Regency medal to be struck, with the date left blank. The King's recovery was infuriating. And indeed, he continued to rule, with occasional lapses, for 22 years more. But a Regency was clearly in prospect, and England looked forward expectantly to the style and verve of a new era.

For England's painters the anticipation of change had an extra dimension. The Prince had proved to be an enthusiastic art lover, and there was every reason to hope that as Regent he would bestow generous royal patronage. Moreover, the art world itself was in transition. At the time of Turner's precocious debut in 1790, Gainsborough had been dead two years and Reynolds had two to live. The giants had had their day; their places would be hard to fill. But they had built well, and art flourished. Thomas Lawrence was making an elegant mark on portraiture. The American expatriates Benjamin West and John Singleton Copley pursued the "grand manner" of history painting. Another notable expatriate was the Swiss master of nightmare and fantasy, Henry Fuseli. Innovation was in the air. Joseph Wright of Derby dramatically employed light and dark in scenes of industry and scientific inquiry. A young Fuseli admirer, William Blake, experimented with color engravings to illustrate his mystical verse. Wilson's landscapes stood challenged by masters of watercolor, from whom Turner would soon learn.

The Royal Academy was by now an institution to be venerated. In its commodious quarters at Somerset House—graciously donated by George III—system and rule prevailed. The Academy had its Professors, Auditors, Visitors, Keeper. Strict regulations governed the student; he could not, for example, draw from the nude female model if he were under 20 and unmarried. There were ritual occasions as well, and notable among them was the periodic delivery of a discourse by Reynolds.

On December 10, 1790, Sir Joshua, 67 and nearly blind, presented his 15th and last discourse before an audience of several hundred. The evening began badly; a beam below the floor gave way and the boards cracked loudly enough to start an exodus. When calm was restored and Reynolds spoke, he could hardly be heard, and bored students in the back chatted among themselves. He went on unheeding. The speech was in the main a review of his devotion to the Academy and to traditional principles of art. His central point concerned what he believed to be the Academy's sole purpose. It was, he declared, to see "that too much indulgence may not be given to peculiarity, and that a young man may not be taught to believe that what is generally good for others is not good for him."

Turner was not likely to have been one of the students who rudely talked while Reynolds discoursed. He was mature beyond his years, and happy to be at the Academy. He had a healthy respect for his elders, and an admiration of Reynolds that was to continue all his life. Nevertheless, it would be he, more than any other painter, who would disprove the worth of Reynolds' advice.

The Prince of Wales's first wife, Maria Fitzherbert, was a London beauty noted for her fine aquiline nose and creamy white bosom, shown to advantage in John Hoppner's oil portrait *(top)*. When Prince George caught sight of the 28-year-old widow in 1784, he fell madly in love. Thomas Rowlandson's ink-and-wash drawing—contrasting her classic profile with the pudgy Prince's nestling posture—suggests that she may have supplied a kind of maternal love to George.

The Adventurous Romantics

Turner and his contemporaries began to look beyond the confines of their native land and their traditional subject matter. Stimulated by the wonders uncovered by explorers, travelers and scholars, English artists conveyed the excitement of their times on canvas and so expanded the boundaries of art and personal expression. To re-create man's past in the light of new archeological knowledge, to capture the moods of nature both dramatically and objectively, to picture the imaginary as real—these became their preoccupations. They were called Romantics. A Romantic painter in London in 1807, for instance, would surely visit Gloucester House to sketch the Classical sculpture recently brought from Greece. If he traveled, he might brave the Alps in hope of finding an avalanche to draw. And listening carefully to new ideas—in philosophy, science, poetry—he found inspiration that closely linked painting and other intellectual pursuits.

Unsatisfied with inherited territory, the Romantic was an explorer. No effort—physical, emotional, mental—was too great: he sailed to the South Seas in search of fresh vistas and traveled in his thoughts even further to find common interest with scientists. If the painter explored, writers were often his guides. Scouring the pages of great literature of the past for heroic and dramatic passages to illustrate, reading contemporary works, the Romantic painter found allies in his search for broader expression. In Romantic art, word and image were companions.

The collaboration among the arts that was so important to the Romantic artist is the theme of this pictorial allegory by the popular woman painter Angelica Kauffmann. Like other works of the period it also celebrates the past: both figures are coiffed and gowned in antique fashion, and Poetry *(right)* holds a Greek lyre. The model for Painting was the artist.

Angelica Kauffmann: *Poetry Embracing Painting*, 1782

The past had always fascinated artists, but the variety and intensity of that interest was never greater than in the century between 1750 and 1850. Poring over such tomes as Stuart's *Antiquities of Athens*, which was illustrated with renderings of Greek temples and statuary, or visiting exhibits of Classical art, English artists sought identification with the glories of past civilizations. The painter Benjamin Haydon, who sketched in meticulous detail the marble sculptures recently imported from the Parthenon *(right)*, also wrote an influential study of their artistic merit.

Other painters let the past retain its mythological, Biblical or legendary character, relying more on imagination than on fact. Perhaps architect Joseph Gandy, whose fantastic *Origins of Architecture* appears below, sought to link his profession with the building of the earth. In natural bridges, dams and spirelike rocks, Gandy found models for all architectural forms.

Joseph Gandy: *Origins of Architecture*, 1838

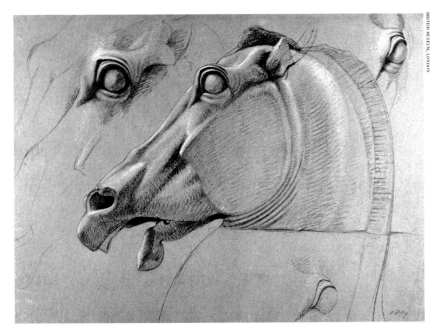

Benjamin Robert Haydon:
Head of the Horse of Selene, 1809

James Barry: *Jupiter and Juno on Mount Ida,* c. 1790-1799

23

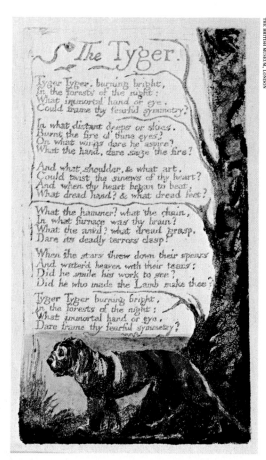

William Blake: *The Tyger*, 1789

William Blake and John Everett Millais represent the chronological extremes of the Romantic era in English art. Yet their fascination with the written word provided models for the entire period. In their paintings below both turned to great literary moments for themes. Blake found in Dante's description of his dead love Beatrice ("... a lady appeared to me, under a green mantle, dressed in the color of flame") one of those drama-filled episodes of which the Romantic imagination was so fond. Millais sought

William Blake: *Beatrice Addressing Dante from the Car*, 1824-1827

inspiration in Shakespeare's description of the drowned Ophelia ("... There with fantastic garlands did she come ...") and created a late Romantic masterpiece.

Painting based on literature became so popular that galleries opened to specialize in just such subjects. Capitalizing on this interest, many Romantic painters paid close attention to the world of literary scholarship, eager to discover original sources for their work. None, however, achieved the success of Blake, whose concern for words

produced a synthesis that had no parallel. In a series of works called Illuminated Books, Blake combined his artistry as an engraver with his talents as a poet and painter. He produced volumes so powerful—from one of which *The Tyger (left)* is taken—that even his own advertisement for them seems modest: "If a method of Printing which combines the Painter and the Poet is a phenomenon worthy of public attention, provided that it exceeds in elegance all former methods, the Author is sure of his reward."

John Everett Millais: *Ophelia*, 1852

To the Romantic imagination the natural world
was more than a stage for human activity; it
seemed to be a force in itself. Painters enlarged this
new, dynamic concept of nature; their emphasis
ranged from strict verisimilitude to imaginative and
emotional interpretation. Various schools of
landscape painting developed, each reflecting a
different aspect of nature's character. Some
considered nature awesome, and often emphasized
its terror: they found in an Alpine avalanche *(far
right)* the sort of cataclysmic event that
overwhelms man by its power. Some thought
nature more serene and found in small, lyric scenes
(right) a truer vision of nature's soul. Other
painters ignored extremes and tried to define for
themselves nature's reality: an abbey decaying in
the Yorkshire hills *(below)*, or the emptiness of a
Norwich heath *(below right)*, seemed to them to
speak just as eloquently of nature's moods and its
effect upon man and his monuments.

Samuel Palmer: *In a Shoreham Garden*, c. 1829

Thomas Girtin: *Kirkstall Abbey, Yorkshire*, 1801

Philip James de Loutherbourg: *An Avalanche in the Alps in the Valley of the Lauterbrunnen*, exhibited 1804

John Crome: *Mousehold Heath, Norwich*, c. 1818-1820

27

William Hodges: *A Crater in the Pacific*, 1772-1775

Joseph Wright (Wright of Derby): *An Experiment on a Bird in the Air Pump*, exhibited 1768

The wedding of art and science was a unique development of the Romantic era. Painters recognized among scientists a passion for investigation and experiment that matched their own. Many kept abreast of scientific activities, and some, like Joseph Wright, found subjects in dramatic moments of research. In the painting at the left below, Wright commemorated a serious amateur's experiment with an air pump—but sympathized with the children's sentimental responses to the struggles of the lark, which died proving that a vacuum had indeed been created.

Other painters actually contributed to scientific research by providing accurate visual records. William Hodges was commissioned by the Royal Navy to accompany Captain Cook's voyage of exploration to the South Seas; his watercolor of a volcano *(left)* is one result. And George Stubbs became so involved in anatomical research that he supplied both the text and drawings for a book comparing the physical structures of animals and humans. In the illustrations below he purposefully exaggerated the similarities between man and owl.

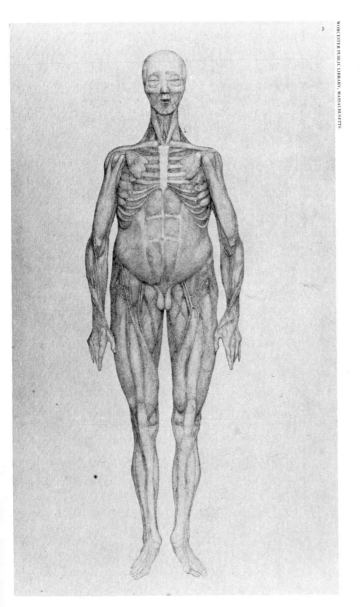

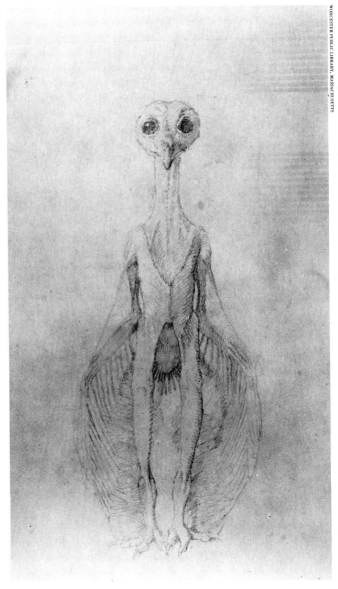

George Stubbs: *Écorché of a Standing Male Figure*, c. 1795-1803

George Stubbs: *The Owl*, c. 1795-1803

Romantic curiosity extended beyond the limits of the physical; at times it probed the mysterious world of the mind. Henry Fuseli's *The Nightmare* is the most sensational example of this interest. No better description of the painting exists than that by the painter's poet-friend Erasmus Darwin, grandfather of the great biologist: "So on his Nightmare, through the evening fog,/Flits the squab Fiend o'er fen, and lake, and bog;/Seeks some love-Wilder'd Maid with sleep oppress'd,/Alights, and, grinning, sets upon her breast." In the scene vision and reality are fused: the demon seems as real, and as frightening, to the observer as it does to the maid whose sleep it disturbs. Whether or not the painting truly foreshadows the later insights of psychoanalysis into the importance of dreams, it is interesting that a copy hung in Sigmund Freud's study.

Fuseli himself was an archetypal Romantic. Swiss-born but London-based, he traveled throughout Western Europe and was the constant companion of poets and philosophers; he not only drew upon literature for most of his paintings but was himself an estimable critic, poet and translator. In all this he saw himself fulfilling the Romantic conviction that art and learning should awaken and deepen human experience.

Henry Fuseli: *The Nightmare*, 1781

31

II

England
Discovers Itself

During Turner's novice years in the early 1790s, the talk of London focused on the violent events of the Revolution in France. Whereas distance had muted the recent American uproar, the bitter clashes of the people versus Louis XVI could be followed at close range. The tremors were quickly felt in England; in time they were to affect its art, and were even to shape the choices open to an obscure young painter.

The response to the tumult across the Channel was at first distinctly sympathetic. Many Englishmen agreed that France's *ancien régime* had asked for its own comeuppance. The fall of its dread prison-fortress, the Bastille, was hailed as a happy augury; no less a personage than the Prince of Wales' playmate and Parliamentary ally, Charles James Fox, pronounced it much the best happening in history. Literary men were equally enthusiastic. Robert Burns, who was a customs officer in his prosier moments, bought up the guns he had seized from a smuggler and, at his own expense, shipped them to the rebels. William Blake sported the French revolutionary's stocking cap around London and wrote his exultant "Song of Liberty." William Wordsworth, fresh from Cambridge, went to sample the French spirit in person.

In this seemingly solid phalanx of favorable opinion the first large crack appeared with *Reflections on the Revolution in France*, by the aging statesman Edmund Burke. Once he had been the spellbinder of the House of Commons; these days his droning orations cleared its benches so swiftly that members dubbed him its dinner bell. But his views still carried weight. The French Revolution, as Burke saw it, was dangerously different from the American Revolution. The Americans, he had felt, were at worst misguided kinsmen; the French were "architects of ruin." By disrupting the social order, they made reform ineffective, for without continuity in everyday affairs, Burke said, human beings were as fated as "flies in a summer."

Reflections brought an answering broadside, *The Rights of Man*, from the fiery propagandist of the American Revolution, Tom Paine. As passionately pro-French as he had been pro-American, he saw their causes as one, and indeed dedicated his essay to President George Washington.

Turner painted only two self-portraits, and exhibited neither of them. He generally had no illusions about his unprepossessing appearance, although in this dandified portrayal, done when he was about 23, he may have succumbed to a bit of self-flattery.

Self-Portrait, c. 1798

Its thesis was startlingly simple: the popular will alone should decide a government's rise or fall. "Paine is no fool," Prime Minister William Pitt remarked in private, "he is perhaps right; but if I did what he wants I should have thousands of bandits on my hands tomorrow, and London burnt."

As the rival arguments crackled, the "Cannibal Republic" Burke had predicted for France seemed nigh. Hope for a constitutional regime dimmed; under new extremist leaders terror stalked the land. In September of 1792 Parisian mobs opened the city's jails and butchered some 1,100 inmates, mostly priests and aristocrats. Four months later Louis XVI was carted off to the guillotine, just one of a bloody processional of "traitors to the Revolution" that would also include his queen, Marie Antoinette, better known to her subjects as "the Austrian bitch." Tom Paine, then in Paris, very nearly lost his own head for protesting the loss of the King's. France's blood bath sent shudders everywhere. "One might as well think," one Englishman wrote, "of establishing a republic of tigers in some forest of Africa."

England was appalled and anxious. The barricades had seasoned a new sort of cocky French soldier; merit, not caste, determined the choice of his officers. A tough, efficiently led army, first formed to defend France against invasion by Prussia and Austria, soon became an invasion force itself. French troops swept into the Lowlands, whose security the English linked with their own. The French envoy to London was ousted; eight days later France replied by declaring war. The date was February 1, 1793; final peace would not come until November 20, 1815, after two strenuous decades in which England's might would be matched against the military genius of a "little corporal" turned dictator, Napoleon Bonaparte.

Among the early casualties of the conflict was the reform movement that had hoped to liberalize English life. In a crackdown on dissidents, Parliament banned public meetings without permit and suspended the right of *habeas corpus*. Sedition trials multiplied. Clubs that had formed in fraternity for the French gave way to groups of vigilantes. In the Lake District, the villagers of Over and Nether Stowey decided that two newcomers to the neighborhood, Wordsworth and his sister Dorothy, were taking too many walks at night, and alerted officials to "French plotters" in their midst. For the lower orders, as for their betters, patriotism was a clear victor over proletarianism.

The war had a direct consequence on the nation's art by denying the English one of their great pleasures. Continental travel was unsafe, and the Grand Tour no longer possible. To generations of the privileged this cherished ritual had given cultural sustenance: contact with the glitter of France, exposure to the treasures of Italy and a look at scenic Switzerland in between. Wealthy travelers often took along painters from home just to record the most stunning vistas. A number of artistic reputations had been built in this fashion. Now the opportunity was gone, and also the chance for the kind of sojourn in Rome that had helped shape the talents of Reynolds and Wilson.

From time to time, however, reminders of Continental delights

As England nervously watched the French Revolution, the engraver and satirist James Gillray took the radical pamphleteer Thomas Paine to task for advocating a dose of republicanism—and even an income tax—at home. Gillray played on the fact that Paine was the son of a small-town corsetmaker. He drew Paine with the ruddy tinge of a drinker, mercilessly lacing up an unhappy Brittania under a shingle proclaiming "Paris modes by express." The caption ran, "A good Constitution sacrificed for a Fantastic Form," and Gillray's upper-crust audience took the warning seriously. They feared intellectuals like Paine, so taken with revolutionary spirit as to foist it on a healthy England.

reached England. One was the sale of the art collection of the Duc d'Or-léans, which had been brought out of France and put on auction. Fashionable London bid generously; even the "refuse" went like wild-fire, one local painter sourly noted. The previous owner was unable to relish the success: under the alias Philippe Egalité he had joined the ranks of the Revolution, voted for the death of his cousin the King, and then had his own head lopped off for his pains.

Other, luckier bluebloods joined a stream of emigrés who sought haven in England, pointedly renting houses by the month to emphasize their expectations of an early return home. Many had known English hospitality in the past, and had proffered theirs in France. But the old sparkle was hard to re-create, all the more so when, as one historian observed, some of the same heads that had smiled in London drawing rooms were now nodding on pikes in Paris.

For the English, it was better to shelve memories and find fresh fields of enjoyment. With the Continent off-limits, the taste for travel had to be indulged in other directions. Barring such outposts as America or the West Indies, the logical place was England itself, and perhaps even Scotland and Wales. At the war's outbreak these two regions were still virtually terra incognita; not long before, Dr. Samuel Johnson, reporting on the Scottish Highlands, had advised that "the uniformity of bar-renness can afford very little amusement." But the Grand Tour had whet-ted the appetite for mountain scenery, and there was yet another parallel to those now forbidden jaunts: in place of Italy's archeological won-ders, the restless Englishman could divert himself with the ruined abbeys and castles that were his own country's proud antiquities.

With these inducements to tempt the traveler, an age of national self-discovery was at hand. The means of getting about the country had vast-ly improved. Until recently, venturing beyond London had been a danger to life and limb. But the perils offered by highwaymen, rutted roads and springless coaches were lessening. Industrialism was forcing a sec-ond revolution in transport. Some 500 turnpike trusts, local companies, were tending the roads in their areas in return for the right to levy tolls. Lighter, faster and more comfortable stagecoaches were being built. Travelers who preferred the privacy of a post chaise, hiring hors-es from town to town, could count on better service at the coaching-inns. In the last decade of the 18th Century, a day's journey could cover about a hundred miles, twice as much as in midcentury.

The countryside was ripe for inspection. Much of the wilderness had been cleared, and the landscape was acquiring a neater look, with fenced fields and ordered hedgerows. The disfiguring marks of industrialism were still few. As the historian Trevelyan put it, England was "at her best, at the perfect moment before the outrages on her beauty began." The younger landscape painters, Turner among them, stood ready to me-morialize that moment.

The English traveler, like the rubbernecking tourist of a later day, craved souvenirs of his sightseeing. The 18th Century equivalent of the postcard or snapshot was the topographical drawing, the precise ren-dering of manmade or natural landmarks. In deft hands topography—

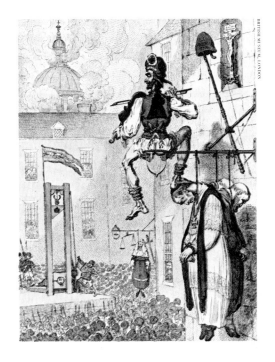

The beheading of Louis XVI on January 21, 1793, shocked Englishmen, and with it virtually all popular sympathy for the Revolution died. Gillray expressed his countrymen's dismay with a gruesome drawing of the regicide, showing Louis pinioned in the guillotine with his crown tied to the blade above him, while clerics and a judge hang lifelessly from street lamps. A gamy revolutionary perched on one of the lamps fiddles while Paris burns. "The zenith of French glory," Gillray called it, adding, "Religion, Justice, Loyalty . . . Farewell!"

in effect, the portraiture of places—could be quick work, and its practitioners found willing patrons among England's stylish sightseers.

Until shortly before Turner's time topographical drawing had been considered less an art than a kind of adjunct to map making. A map of one of England's counties, for example, might be decorated around the borders with accurately scaled views of the area's historical sites, of prominent natural phenomena or of well-known stately homes. Then in the 1770s topographical drawing as an art form got an unexpected boost from an unlikely source: Catherine the Great of Russia. As avid a collector of curiosa as of lovers, the Empress ordered a china tea service from England's newly famous potter, Josiah Wedgwood, stipulating that each piece—952 in all—carry a different English view. Wedgwood gamely scouted the scenic possibilities and rustled up enough material to complete the order within two years. Before shipment to St. Petersburg, Catherine's elaborate whimsy was displayed in London, and it stirred both a sensation and some fresh ideas of topography's worth.

Its full acceptance as an art, however, came only as it began to be identified with individual talents. More and more, painters went out on their own, choosing views themselves. Traditionally, topographical views were supposed to be objective, accurately rendered without interpretive comment. Yet no artist worth his salt could conceal his touch. Paul Sandby, the venerable dean of topographers in Turner's youth, had been trained in the most rigorous branch of his technique, as a draftsman on a government survey expedition to Scotland. But the views he drew when on leave in Edinburgh and on subsequent sketching tours betrayed such subjective accents as the loving concentration on an ancient tree. Judged by the expressiveness of later landscape art, Sandby's work seems passionless. But it suggested topography's potential, and when the Royal Academy was launched, Sandby's presence among its founders—most of them portraitists—occasioned no surprise.

Closely connected with the rise of topography as an art was the growing use of watercolors. Earlier topographers had been timid about color, venturing just a tint here and there over their drawings. Sandby was bolder, and his experiments spurred others, who carried the art far beyond the confining limits of topography. The watercolor medium proved subtler and more versatile than anyone had dreamed.

Watercolors were eventually to be known in Europe as *l'art anglais*, in recognition of the special English flair for the medium. Various reasons have been advanced for this, among them that the pale tones and soft contrasts of watercolor are unusually suited to record the delicate qualities of England's landscape and to reflect the vagaries of its moist climate. Whatever the case, the work of the English watercolorists came to be unmistakable. Out of the three homely ingredients of paper and water and colors were wrought marvels of jewel-like purity, almost like miniature stained-glass windows in their quiet glow and authority.

The early watercolorists hoped to raise their medium to a par with oil painting, to prove that the one could be as imaginative and as expressive as the other. They drew strength for this cause from two remarkable artists, the Russian-born Alexander Cozens and his son John

A view of a castle in Gloucestershire decorates this dinner plate created by the noted potter Josiah Wedgwood for Catherine the Great in 1774. Russia's extravagant empress ordered a service of 952 pieces, each painted with a different landscape, under a shield with a frog. (Her St. Petersburg palace was called *La Grenouille*—The Frog). Wedgwood dispatched artists all over the British Isles to sketch the scenes, spending two years on the project and inadvertently helping to make landscape art fashionable. Most of the china, which survived Catherine's demise and the Russian Revolution, still reposes in St. Petersburg (now Leningrad), at the Hermitage Museum.

36

Robert. Alexander was widely reputed to be the son of Peter the Great by the wife of an English shipbuilder whom the late Czar had employed. Of more lasting interest to Alexander's colleagues, however, was his belief that an artist should give free play to his creative instincts. Generally uninterested in strict topographical views, he argued that the artist could construct a landscape as absorbing as any in nature by dropping blots of ink on paper, crumpling the paper to smear the ink and then letting his brush roam over the random result to complete the work. In that pre-Rorschach era there were those in London who gibed at Alexander as "blotmaster to the town," but the watercolorists were fascinated.

The essence of the blot theory was its attack on the limitations of literalness. John Robert Cozens' landscapes were identifiable, but invested with a strong sense of the artist's presence and mood. The mood was almost always melancholic; John Robert was subject to depressions, and did, in fact, die insane. The watercolors he produced, in brooding blues, grays and greens, were odes to the silence and solitude in nature. To the younger men who studied them the lesson was clear. The art of landscape need not be restricted to faithful representation; it could be a challenging experience in self-expression as well.

Both the topographical and the interpretive philosophies of landscape were in vogue when Turner began his apprenticeship in the 1790s. From each fount he was to drink deep; he had a limitless thirst for the knowledge of art. He was also a glutton for work. Copying from antique plaster casts and making life-studies of the nude at the Royal Academy took but part of his time. More practical kinds of education were to be had elsewhere. At drawing classes run by Thomas Malton, a Sandby admirer who specialized in architectural views, Turner mastered perspective. At the shop of the engraver J. R. Smith, a few doors down from the Turner home in Maiden Lane, he earned while he learned. For a shilling or two per session he colored prints, acquiring the difficult knack of laying in the color washes carefully and evenly.

When he was 20 or 21, Turner thought to add to his income by taking on a few pupils of his own; but although he was an ideal student himself, he proved to be the poorest of teachers. Inarticulate then as in later life, he had trouble explaining what he wanted and was too impatient to try. As a result, complained one disgruntled pupil, Turner ended up leaving his students entirely alone. Inevitably, the teaching experiment failed badly.

A more fruitful experience was provided by a prominent London physician named Thomas Monro. Dr. Monro, like his father and grandfather before him, was a specialist in mental ills, one of the many doctors who attended George III. (He was also friendly enough with the Prince of Wales to play court tennis with him, incurring an injury that permanently lamed him.) Another Monro patient was John Robert Cozens, then in his final demented state. The Cozens case was probably most to the doctor's liking, for when he was not pursuing his practice he was relentlessly pursuing art. Such was his addiction that he had a netting built into the roof of his carriage to hold drawings, so they would always be handy for scrutiny when he traveled between town and country.

In London, Dr. Monro lived at Adelphi Terrace, a large, exclusive complex of houses that had recently been built on the banks of the Thames. Horace Walpole detested its architecture; it reminded him of "warehouses laced down the seams like a soldier's trull in a regimental old coat." But to Turner, who spent many winter evenings at Dr. Monro's over a period of about three years, the candlelit elegance of the surroundings was a world away from his bleak attic bedroom; and his host's collection of paintings and drawings—including Gainsboroughs, Wilsons and Canalettos—was a revelation.

Benevolence and shrewdness, in equal parts, seem to have motivated Dr. Monro in inviting Turner, along with a number of other young artists, to his home. He had many of Cozens' drawings, finished and unfinished, that he wanted copied, and for half-a-crown and an oyster supper Turner and the others were glad to oblige. A sketch of Turner at one of these sessions, made by Dr. Monro, survives. It shows a solemn-faced youth at work with a pen, his dress indifferent and his straggly hair no credit to a barber's son.

At Dr. Monro's, Turner cemented a friendship with a fellow artist whose death a few years later would snuff out a major talent. Thomas Girtin was two months older than Turner and, like him, a Londoner to the core, born in Great Bandy Leg Walk in Southwark. They had sat side by side coloring prints at J. R. Smith's engraving shop, and in copying Cozens' watercolors for Dr. Monro they often worked as a team.

But in person they were poles apart—Turner undersized, awkward, deadly serious; Girtin handsome, outgoing, ever ready to roister. While Turner plugged away at improving his technical proficiency, Girtin's approach was easy and relaxed. This showed not only in a broad self-assurance—one of his later projects was a 1,944-square-foot panoramic view of London—but also in the look of his work. Girtin's generous eye saw nature at its most sweeping and spacious. In his watercolors the forms are massive and elemental and the foregrounds uncluttered. Meticulous detail plainly bored him, whether he was painting a mountain view in his favorite sketching region, Yorkshire, or a view of the low-lying lands around London. Thus, the true subject of a Yorkshire scene painted in 1800, *Kirkstall Abbey (page 26)*, is not the abbey itself but the sweep and softness of the rolling country around it. Girtin's *White House*, a watercolor of a small cottage nestling against the Chelsea shoreline, is a masterpiece of nature made simpler, almost abstract in its understatement.

Influential even in his brief lifetime, Girtin's art might well have surpassed Turner's if its bold vision had been allowed to develop further. Turner himself sensed this and indeed acknowledged it. Looking back, years after Girtin had died of a lung ailment at 27, he told a colleague: "Had Tom lived I should have starved."

In economic terms, at least, the comment was far-fetched. Turner was too tireless and too canny to fail to reap substantial gain from his labors. From the beginning he directed his efforts where they would do his pocket the most good. The theory that art and commercial success

This sketch of the young Turner working intently by candlelight was made by Dr. Thomas Monro around 1795. The physician's fashionable practice was devoted to the mentally ill (he prescribed a pillow of hop fiber for George III's lunacy), but his evenings were devoted to young artists. He made a studio of his London townhouse, inviting talented youths to copy the watercolors in his collection. Turner sometimes merely added color and shading to outlines drawn by other Monro protégés. As the years passed, some of these men became famous—and their work for their old patron went on sale. Turner was so upset at seeing the market flooded with these early efforts that he bought up hundreds of them himself to take them out of circulation.

are inimical would have astonished him. While fiercely asserting his right to self-expression, he frankly regarded his work as a business.

The most lucrative products for a young artist at the time were topographical views that could be reproduced as engravings. These were extremely popular both as magazine features and in the form of folios made up of a dozen or so related prints grouped under such titles as *Picturesque Views of the Antiquities of England and Wales* and *Select Views of Gentlemen's Seats*. This link with the publishing world promised an artist a way to further his fame and, if he applied himself, his fortune. Turner, for one, took the cue early and never forgot it. In large part his reputation and wealth were built on the stupendous number of his works that were circulated in reproduction—a total of 900 separate prints, some selling thousands of copies.

Turner achieved this extraordinary output by starting, early on, a lifelong habit of summer sketching tours. The very words have a romantic ring, conjuring up casual rambles and sudden joys of discovery. Turner's tours, however, were as purposeful as a salesman's and as persistent: he made his first when he was 16 and his last when he was 70. Within the first decade after his enrollment at the Academy he had covered most of England and Wales, by stagecoach, on horseback or on foot, sometimes walking 30 miles a day. Everything was grist for his mill: a desolate abbey, a cathedral close, an old town wall, farmhouses, jetties, all the monuments of man raised against the monuments of nature—hill and dale and mountain and sea.

He traveled light, with little more than a change of linen, an umbrella, a flute for the rare idle moments and, of course, the tools of his trade; one boon was the recent development of solid cakes of color, which were easier and less messy to carry than the old liquid pigments. Occasionally he had the company of a fellow artist—Girtin was one—but more often he went alone. At night he put up at the nearest inn. One companion recalled Turner asleep upright on a taproom bench after a light supper of cheese and ale. But he was seldom too weary to work up the day's pencilings, going over them with pen or brush, and adding touches of color.

His sketchbooks, now treasured by the British Museum, indicate Turner was gaining a growing mastery of his art; they also reveal a good deal about his character. Jottings of the distances between points on his itinerary and notations about the towns to be visited reflect his methodical bent. Even the bindings tell a story. The first sketchbooks have simple cardboard covers, but soon Turner covered them in calf with brass hinges—the better to impress potential patrons.

That patrons were indeed showing heightened interest in Turner's offerings is evidenced by his lists of "order'd drawings," and the sharp rise in their prices. In 1795 Turner charged two guineas for a drawing, but by 1799 he could command as high as 40 guineas, about as much as a country curate earned in a year. Some of these profitable commissions were from publishers. He produced a number of drawings for the *Copper Plate Magazine*, a self-styled "monthly treasure for the admirers of the imitative arts," and for another monthly, the aptly named *Pocket*

Magazine, which measured about three by five inches. A view of Bristol, signed W. Turner, appeared in its October 1795 issue, immediately followed by an article on making potato bread. It is doubtful that the juxtaposition bothered Turner in the least.

A glimpse of him on his early travels was provided long afterward by a niece of a Bristol dealer in hides, John Narraway, a family friend whose home Turner sometimes thriftily used as a base for his forays into Wales. From her account it would seem that he was not much fun to have around: crude in manners, silent at table, averse to song or games, out sketching before breakfast and after dinner. Behind his back the Narraways called him the "Prince of the Rocks" for the way he haunted the cliffs above the River Avon. They also found him "somewhat mean and ungrateful," but he could be self-deprecating. Once, asked to paint his own portrait, he said, "It will do my drawings an injury, people will say such a little fellow as this can never draw."

Nevertheless he subsequently produced two self-portraits, the first in watercolor, the second in oil *(page 32).* The latter shows him at about 23, rather more dandified and attractive than he was ever to appear in anyone else's portrait of him. The eyes are the most distinctive feature. They gaze directly at the viewer and yet beyond him, as if fixed on the promise of the future.

Even in the optimism of youth, however, Turner was not one to hurry the future. If he dreamed of setting the world on fire, he also sensed the need to build step by step. In his first years as an exhibitor at the Academy—the major showcase of an artist's progress—he was plainly not out to make a splash. The works he displayed, all watercolors, were dexterously executed but unoriginal; their debt to the topographical teachings of Sandby and Malton was evident. Such subjects as *View of the River Avon near St. Vincent's Rock, Bristol; Christ Church Gate, Canterbury; St. Hughe the Burgundian's Porch at Lincoln Cathedral;* and *Marford Mill, Wrexham, Denbighshire* were clearly the products of a painter content with convention, and therefore eminently acceptable to the Academy's hanging committee.

In the mid-1790s, Turner's individuality seemed suddenly to flower. His entries at the Academy were more personal and inventive. Some watercolors employed bright yellows and Venetian reds alongside the customary blues and grays, and all the colors were laid on with an unusual delicacy of touch—the first sign of the gift that Constable admired when, many years later, he described Turner's colors as "tinted steam." There was also evidence of a new absorption in light and shade. Turner's *Transept of Ewenny Priory, Glamorganshire* is a dramatic study in gloom offset by a few shafts of sunlight. The careful architectural details are there, but this is no longer mere topography. With its exaggeratedly oblique vantage point and its moody contrasts of light and dark, the scene is imaginatively transformed.

The same imaginative quality also began to emerge in Turner's oils. Initially, he seems to have been diffident about this medium. He waited until 1796, his seventh year as an Academy exhibitor, to enter an oil, and then only one, with 10 watercolors to bolster it. This picture was called *Fishermen at Sea*, and Turner need not have fretted over its reception. It won him a spectacular bouquet in the press. A few critics had previously noted his promise, but the author of the present review was the terror of creative London, the snarling, satirical John Williams, who was forever enmeshed in quarrels and libels and who was soon, to everyone's relief, to depart for America. One of his publications, written under the pseudonym of Anthony Pasquin, was a *Critical Guide* to the 1796 Academy show. It not only commended Turner's painting "to the judicious," but added: "It is managed in a manner somewhat novel, yet the principle of that management is just: we do not hesitate in affirming that this is one of the greatest proofs of an original mind in the present pictorial display: the boats are buoyant and swim well, and the undulation of the element is admirably deceiving."

The comment is memorable not only because it announced Turner's arrival as an oil painter, but also because it forecast the pattern of criticism that was to evolve around his work: a tinge of unease at its novelty, yet a recognition of mastery. It was becoming clear now that nature's attraction for Turner lay in its elemental forces. More and more, as he tramped the country he found his excitement and his challenge in its mountains and seas, and in the squalls and storms and ominous calms through which they spoke nature's voice. As these themes increasingly preoccupied him, they began to appear among his Academy offerings: in 1797, *Fishermen coming ashore at sunset, previous to a gale;* in 1798, *Dunstanburgh Castle, N. E. coast of Northumbria. Sunrise after a squally night;* in 1799, *Kilgarran castle on the Twyvey, hazy sunrise, previous to a sultry day.* The power of his imagination was loosed, and would never again be caged.

Among his entries for the 1799 exhibition, Turner submitted an oil of a very different sort, an expression not so much of individuality as of patriotism. The painting, *Battle of the Nile*, was later lost, and in any event the canvas itself was of less moment than the bit of history that inspired it. The summer before, at Aboukir Bay in Egypt, Admiral Horatio Nelson had trapped a French fleet accompanying Napoleon on his campaign to conquer the Levant. All but two of the 13 French men-of-war were destroyed, and Napoleon himself was temporarily left high and dry. Most important, the Mediterranean, which he had recently and jarringly described as a "French Lake," was back in England's control.

The English had badly needed the victory. In five years of war, successes in battle had been few, and none at all had been won on land: the Continent remained Napoleon's. There had been other troubles as well: the breakup of a European coalition that England had forged against France, a rebellion among the Catholics of Ireland and, at home, the imposition of an income tax to help pay the cost of war. George III wandered in a deepening twilight, able to enjoy only dimly a new personal popularity caused by his subjects' revulsion against the Revolution's treatment of Louis XVI.

The popularity of the Prince of Wales, on the other hand, had been in a steady decline. His irresponsibility and wanton ways had made him distrusted even by a public inclined to be indulgent of royal philandering; his carriage could not go through London without being pelted. In 1794 he had deserted Maria Fitzherbert and agreed to marry a slovenly, loud-mouthed German princess, Caroline of Brunswick, with the understanding that his father would cancel his debts, then standing at some £400,000. The first sight of his bride had sent him to the brandy bottle, and he had turned up drunk for the ceremony. A daughter, Charlotte, was born of this union, but the Prince and Princess were soon estranged. He had a new mistress, Lady Jersey, a witty and elegant grandmother of 42, and a new crony and fashion oracle: the exquisitely groomed Beau Brummell, a valet's grandson turned social climber, who took an hour every day just to inch into his skintight breeches.

More solid citizens longed for something to take away the taste of defeat abroad and decadence at home, and they found it in Nelson's coup at Aboukir Bay. Its celebration by the painters—Turner's canvas was one of four on the subject at the same Academy show—reflected a widespread optimism. Although Napoleon had slipped through the Mediterranean patrols and returned home to continue his course of conquest, there were grounds for encouragement. Nelson's victory had restored allies to the English camp. A second coalition, with Russia and Austria, was under way. In 1799 the attitude of the English was hopeful. A change for the better seemed imminent.

For Turner, too, the year spelled change—in his private as well as professional affairs. He decided to leave home; his mother's increasingly demented tantrums made it impossible to concentrate, and so he rented lodgings in Harley Street. The rooms were larger and better lighted than in the house in Maiden Lane, and the neighborhood was more desirable. The move had another advantage in that it gave Turner the freedom to come and go without parental prying. He had a new reason for wanting that freedom: the lively Sarah Danby, a widow with four small children, who lived not far off, near Fitzroy Square.

So far as is known she was Turner's first love. Her husband, John Danby, had been a musician of some repute who had served as organist at the chapel of the Spanish Embassy, composing some of its masses and motets; he had also written a number of much-admired glees. Turner, among other artists, was interested in Danby's music and presumably was taken with the young widow while offering his condolences.

Professionally he also prospered. Commissions poured in from publishers as well as from wealthy patrons. The Earl of Elgin, appointed envoy to the Ottoman Empire, asked him to go along to sketch the antiquities of Greece, then under Turkish control. His Lordship, however, was a hard bargainer: he specified not only that he acquire the rights to all the sketches, but that Turner give Lady Elgin drawing lessons in his off-hours. When Turner set a value of £400 a year on these services, Lord Elgin promptly broke off negotiations. Turner was thus spared a share in one of art history's most famous imbroglios. While pursuing the antique, the Earl got the Sultan's permission to remove from the Acropolis in Athens "any pieces of stone with old inscriptions or figures thereon." Exercising that permission vigorously, he permanently enriched the English—and enraged the Greeks—by dismantling and

The Prince of Wales's engagement to Caroline of the German House of Brunswick inspired this irreverent view by James Gillray. The sleeping Prince is being tendered £150,000 for good behavior by his father as his mother proffers a book titled *The Art of Getting Pretty Children*. His fiancée, accompanied by the light of love, banishes the shades of the Prince's profligate bachelorhood. Prince George was not amused by Gillray's jibes, and later had him clapped in jail for another cartoon. But London's smart set queued up in Bond Street to buy Gillray's engravings.

sending home the incalculable treasure of the so-called Elgin Marbles.

Turner found a more congenial spirit in the millionaire dilettante William Beckford. Beckford's taste in art had been shaped largely by the Cozens, father and son; John Robert had served as his draftsman on the Grand Tour. On his own, Beckford had acquired other tastes such as traveling with a hired harpsichordist, delving into exotic Orientalia and writing romantic novels; he wrote one, *Vathek*, in French, at a single feverish sitting of three days and two nights. His dearest hobby, however, was Fonthill Abbey, a medieval-style monstrosity with a tower nearly 300 feet high, that he was having built on the family estate in Wiltshire. Naturally, Beckford wanted the progress recorded in pictures, and he had enlisted, among other artists, Reynolds' successor as Academy president, Benjamin West. Turner was also asked to join the company, and he produced several watercolors of the Abbey from various vantages, all mercifully remote.

Of more importance to Turner's art, the contact with Beckford gave the young painter his first look at the works of Claude, and planted in him a lifelong admiration for the French master. The paintings that so impressed Turner were two landscapes that came into Beckford's hands after an intriguing sequence of adventures. Two Englishmen in Rome had bought them from a blind Italian nobleman, Prince Altieri, and, a step ahead of Napoleon's invading troops, had carried them by wagon to Naples, by boat to Palermo, and thence, with a personal letter of safe conduct from Admiral Nelson, to Gibraltar. There the paintings were put aboard a small armed vessel, the *Tiger*, which carried its cargo safely to Falmouth despite pursuit by enemy ships. Beckford purchased the Altieri Claudes and put them on view at his London town house. Turner twice went to see them. His reaction to one of the paintings, *The Sacrifice of Apollo*, was noted in Farington's diary. Turner, he wrote, "was both pleased and unhappy while he viewed it, it seemed to be beyond the power of imitation."

The Beckford showing provided a further footnote to art history. Among the other guests was John Constable. At this first encounter of the two future giants of English landscape painting—Turner just 24, Constable soon to be 23—the pleasantries exchanged are unrecorded. The men were altogether dissimilar. Constable, handsome and easygoing, was just up from the country, having finally convinced his father, a Suffolk grain merchant, to let him pursue the painter's life. He was at the very beginning of his career in art and, at the time of meeting Turner, was awaiting admission as an Academy student.

Turner, for his part, was about to reach a milestone in his career that Constable would take two more decades to achieve. On November 4, 1799, he was elected an Associate of the Academy, one of an elite 20 who stood just below the highest rank of Academician. The ceremony of induction took place on December 31, on the very eve of a new year and a new century. So far as his colleagues could tell, Turner was destined to be a great credit to the artistic establishment. There was some talk of his "new developments" in landscape painting, but it was approving talk. Before long the tone would grow chilly.

When Turner's friend and patron William Beckford commissioned Fonthill Abbey in 1795, he planned a "folly"—a replica of a Gothic ruin designed merely as an ornament for his estate. But he became so enchanted by the project that he kept building until he had completed a permanent residence. It took five years and cost a quarter of a million pounds—approximately five million dollars in today's terms. Fonthill was a chaos of composition. Cross-shaped, it covered six acres and contained, among other extravagances, a tower, cloisters, choir and gallery, like those of a medieval abbey. Its Great Hall, hung with crimson silks, rose 120 feet and was impossible to heat—although much perfumed coal was consumed in the attempt. In 1826 the tower collapsed, making Fonthill the picturesque ruin Beckford had first envisioned.

During much of Turner's life, England's great political issue was Parliamentary reform. At the end of the 18th Century, representation in Parliament was still limited by 15th Century voting laws based on obsolete political boundaries. Thousands in the new industrial cities had no franchise whatever, while a handful of voters in a village might send two members to the House of Commons. The election process was often a formality, at which candidates nominated by aristocratic landowners could be voted into office by a show of hands; when electors were actually polled, corrupt officials and armed soldiers made sure they voted "correctly." The movement to reform these inequities had gone on for decades, but when peace returned after the English defeated Napoleon in 1815, it gained momentum. In 1827, Benjamin Haydon, a colleague of Turner's, was moved to inject Reform politics into his work. The improvident Haydon had been thrown into a debtors' prison; while there, he watched the prisoners, who were allowed an unusual amount of freedom, put on a charade of a free, Reform election. Haydon was so struck by the fervor and high spirits of the mock election that, after leaving prison, he painted the scene. On the following pages are details from Haydon's *Chairing the Members (below right)*, showing prisoners acting out the passion—and apathy—toward Reform that was being felt in the country at large. As the artist wrote, "What is the world but a prison of larger dimensions?"

Spirits of Reform

Artist Benjamin Haydon looks down on the courtyard of King's Bench Prison, where prisoners have just held a Parliamentary "election." The mock "High Sheriff" wards off three guards, while other voters rally around the two "Members of Parliament" they have chosen and want to "chair"—carry aloft in triumph.

A detachment of Grenadier Guards was called to King's Bench to back up prison turnkeys trying to stop the celebration. The prisoners, however, loudly and actively protested the presence of troops. Led by the "High Sheriff," center, the demonstrators included a prisoner's visiting son, a tyke on whose tin sword hung the motto

"Freedom of Election." The "Lord Mayor" stands at the right of the Guards, according to Haydon's notes, his "hand on heart with mock gravity and . . . indignation at this violation of Magna Charta and civil rights." The elderly man at right, once a fine gentleman, went mad despairing of freedom, Haydon said.

That not everyone cared to agitate for Reform was apparent after the Guards arrived. Cowering under a curtain, one prisoner (lower left) prefers silence. Yet the demonstration, top, indicates that most prisoners "wish for their rights, and their rights they will have"; some of their demands appear on the prison walls (details

above). The scene amuses a Guardsman and his Sergeant (center right). For while the "chairing" is going on, so are the amenities of this debtors' prison. In evidence are such delicacies as wine and pineapples (opposite). At an upper window, a lady smokes a water pipe; at lower left, his children visit a sozzled prisoner.

One of the elected prisoners (center left) actually believed he would be seated in Parliament. Caught up in the charade, he used a champagne glass to belabor a prison guard who tried to halt his victory procession. The second "Member" wearing a feathered Spanish hat, knew the proceedings were a farce but vocifer-

ously denounced the soldiers' entering a place of voting. The well-publicized frolic at King's Bench Prison
was one added bit of fuel for the Reform fire. Within five years, the government passed its first Reform Bill;
in Turner's day "chairing" of duly elected representatives of the people began to take on real meaning.

III

Constable and Turner: Two Views of Nature

At about the same time that Turner painted his self-portrait (*page 32*), John Constable sat for his friend R. R. Reinagle, a fellow landscapist with whom he shared rooms in London. The 23-year-old Constable later fell out with Reinagle, both because of a dispute they had about a picture they jointly owned and because Constable found Reinagle a too-slavish imitator of the artistic styles of the past.

Richard Ramsay Reinagle:
Portrait of Constable, c. 1798

At the start of the 19th Century London was as much a magnet for painters as Paris would be a hundred years later. Life was comfortable and convivial; no signs of the war obtruded. In fashionable drawing rooms the news that the Prince of Wales had gone back to Mrs. Fitzherbert stirred more ripples than did Napoleon's rout of the Austrians at Marengo. Except at sea, the battles with France were being fought by other peoples' sons on other peoples' territories. Secure in their island isolation, the English pursued business-as-usual. The pace was unhurried; there was ample time and money for the arts. A bright prospect awaited the young painter with even a modicum of drive.

Turner had this quality in excess; not so Constable. The thought of having to hustle for one's fame repelled him; his country boy instincts balked at the city's ways. Although drawn there by the urge to excel, he felt out of his depth. "It is difficult to find a man in London possessing even common honesty," he wrote bitterly, and with good cause: his roommate, a fellow student at the Academy, had bilked him of his share of the resale of a Ruisdael landscape they had jointly bought for copying. Thereafter Constable elected to live alone, seeking trusted older men to steer him through London's shoals. Unlike the sturdily self-reliant Turner, he was singularly immature for his mid-20s. He was, in fact, to reach 40 before he emerged from what one chronicler described as "a state of dreamy adolescence."

Among the counselors he found was Turner's friend, Joseph Farington, who seemed to know everyone and everything to do with the art world. Himself a painter who had profited little from studying with Richard Wilson, Farington had an eye for the faults of others. In Constable's flounderings he detected a tendency toward anxious imitation of the Dutch. "I recommended him to study nature, and particular art less," Farington noted in his diary. He had more tangible advice, too. Constable seemed to want to paint only for pleasure, indifferent to the tastes of potential buyers and ignorant of what to charge when one actually turned up; Farington had to caution him not to accept less than 10 guineas for a landscape for which he had been ready to take three.

When another mentor, J. T. Smith, an engraver who had used some Constable sketches of country cottages, offered to put his works on sale in his shopwindow, Farington was aghast. So vulgar a ploy was altogether the wrong way into art's inner circles.

Constable found a more seemly entree under the wing of the celebrated collector Sir George Beaumont, whose mother lived near the Constables in Suffolk. One of London's leading tastemakers, the opinionated Sir George was famous for his dictum that "a good picture, like a good fiddle, should be brown." Constable would one day summon up the gumption to place a violin on the grass and confront Sir George with the contrast, but such *lèse majesté* would have been unthinkable when they first met. Gratefully Constable accompanied his sponsor to private showings and social evenings with artist friends. Moreover, he had the run of the fine Beaumont collection, studying and copying its Claudes and its Girtin watercolors.

This brought Constable some satisfaction, but London itself remained hard to take. It was noisy, crowded and—worst of all—sooty. Looking at the sky, he complained, was like viewing "a pearl through a burnt glass." He missed Suffolk, and went back when he could. He also made two sketching tours, to the Peak District and to the Lake District in the north of England, two scenic areas considered a must for every landscape artist to visit. Their net effect was to satisfy Constable that there was no place like home. For the rest of his years he remained convinced that in and around his own birthplace of East Bergholt there were vistas enough for any painter. "The beauty of the surrounding scenery," he wrote late in life, "its gentle declivities, its luxuriant meadow flats sprinkled with flocks and herds, its well-cultivated uplands, its woods and rivers, with numerous scattered villages and churches, farms and picturesque cottages, all impart to this particular spot an amenity and elegance hardly anywhere else to be found."

And so, whenever Constable could get away from his studies in London, he went home. If his father was still frosty about his career, his mother doted on him, and there was fond admiration from his brothers Golding and Abram, his sisters Mary, Ann and Martha. The Constables owned a large brick Georgian house on 37 acres commanding the River Stour and Dedham Vale. The fields and lanes always beckoned, and Constable continued a boyhood habit of tramping and sketching them with John Dunthorne, the village plumber and an amateur painter. There were commissions, too: portraits of the gentry, well-to-do farmers, relatives. Portraiture, Constable felt privately, was potboiling, but at least it established his credentials. It also helped thaw his father, who relented so far as to buy him a cottage in East Bergholt as a studio.

When painting palled, the social calendar offered its sedate pleasures: tea with the dowager Lady Beaumont, a call on the Reverend Dr. Durand Rhudde at the rectory, dances at which the local girls were delighted to see that the "handsome miller," muscular and fresh-skinned, was quite unspoiled by London. Having to go back there was always a wrench, and the Constables did what they could to ease his lot. By friends going to the city his mother sent baskets of country fare, cambric shirts, a "mite" of money to pad his allowance. No favor he asked was too much; when he wrote requesting a woodpecker, presumably to use as a model, his brother Golding went out and shot one for him.

There must have been times when Constable would have gladly chucked London altogether. In 1802 his first painting at an Academy exhibition, entitled simply *Landscape*, went unnoticed. He considered a proffered post as drawing master at the royal military school at Windsor, but Benjamin West, then president of the Academy, warned him that it would prove a professional dead end. He had, in fact, no tangible evidence to suggest that his painting would ever lead elsewhere, yet he had a stubborn pride and was determined to hang on.

Constable also made an important decision concerning the direction his art would take in the future. Many of his fellow artists, he concluded after three years' observation, were "reprobates," mercenary types who went at their canvases without feeling and who produced "cold, trumpery stuff" as a result. He, too, had been guilty of error: "I have been running after pictures, and seeking the truth at second hand," he wrote Dunthorne in 1802. "I have not endeavoured to represent nature with the same elevation of mind with which I set out, but have rather tried to make my performances look like the work of other men. . . . *There is room enough for a natural painter,*" he continued prophetically. "The great vice of the present day is *bravura*, an attempt to do something beyond the truth. Fashion always had, and will have, its day; but truth in all things only will last."

But more than a decade would pass before any success marked Constable's pursuit of truth in art. In the meantime, as he had noted, fashion was having its day, and fashion dictated that landscape painters seek in nature not truth but drama. As the painter Henry Fuseli put it in an Academy lecture, "the tame delineation of a given spot" was the least interesting of approaches. The knowing artist celebrated nature not through its commonplaces but through its grandeurs. It was a formula that had worked well for the old masters, and was still working well, a sure way to win the plaudits of critics and patrons.

If Constable could not accept this formula, Turner took full advantage of it. The oils he entered in the early Academy shows of the new century met the current criteria: subjects suitable, conceptions grand, homage to past principles plain. Yet his paintings—among them *The Fifth Plague of Egypt, Dutch Boats in a Gale* and *Fishermen upon a Lee Shore in Squally Weather*—showed a vigorous brushwork and a stunning theatricality of lighting that was new, suggesting a fresh idea of what historical landscapes and marine views could be. One critic complained that Turner's rendering was much too "indeterminate and wild," but such demurrers were lost in the general acclaim. Turner's colleagues buzzed with the news that the collector William Beckford had paid 150 guineas for the *Fifth Plague*—as much as Sir Joshua Reynolds had ever received for a portrait—and that the Duke of Bridgewater, the Croesus of coal mines and canal building, had paid 250 for *Dutch Boats*. In February of 1802 the Academy gave Turner its ultimate accolade: election to the rank of Academician, attested by a diploma personally signed by

George III. Turner was not yet 27 years old, and next to Thomas Lawrence he was the youngest man in Academy history to have attained that eminence.

Spreading fame brought Turner all the work he could handle. In addition to painting he was furnishing watercolor sketches for Oxford University's *Almanack*, a calendar that had been in continuous publication since 1676; he was doing sketches for the *Magna Britannia*, a projected five-volume compendium of information about every English parish; and he was working up material from a three-week tour of Scotland he had made in the summer of 1801. In whatever spare time he had Turner was reading the poets, one of the many gaps to be filled in his education now that he was moving among cultivated men. He was also wrestling with French grammar, a study he would soon have a chance to put to practical use.

In March of 1802, in the northern French city of Amiens, England and France signed a treaty of peace. Napoleon wanted to consolidate his gains; the English wanted to be done with war. So strong was this sentiment that London crowds welcomed a French envoy by pulling his carriage through the streets. But the cheering stopped when the peace terms were published. England, mainly because of inept negotiations, had given up almost all its wartime conquests, and for nothing. Napoleon kept his grip on the strategic Low Countries; worse, he would not open France or any other area he controlled to English trade.

It soon became plain that what was in store was not peace but truce. The enmity was ill concealed. At a Paris reception Napoleon berated the English ambassador; he had not meant to, he later admitted, but "this great gawk . . . put himself in front of my nose." In London, cartoons appeared showing the power-mad "Little Boney," his hat askew, trying to bestride the world. In a jibe at his Corsican ancestry the *Morning Post* added a new epithet—"Mediterranean mulatto."

In little more than a year hostilities resumed, but while the truce lasted it produced one notable bonus: Europe, though closed to England's trade, was open again to its travelers. Foreseeing an influx, Napoleon had the Calais-Paris road repaired. He gauged the English well; they came by the thousands. They swarmed through the palace of Versailles, still beautiful despite its sacking a decade earlier by revolutionary mobs; they snapped up Sèvres china, bronze clocks, inlaid secrétaires. There were novelties to write home about. The fashion in dress was a Grecian style, low cut, with "women from 15 to 70 almost in a state of nature." That reliable remedy for colds, barley sugar, was being sold in the shape of Napoleon's head, laurel wreath and all.

Art lovers found Paris more fascinating than ever. The Louvre, formerly a royal preserve, had just been opened as a national museum. Not only were the works of Poussin and other great native sons on public view for the first time, but there were magnificent new accessions: the spoils of Napoleon's conquests, hauled to Paris by the wagonload and bargeful. From Rome had come the Apollo Belvedere and the Laocoön, nine works by Raphael, two by Correggio; from Florence, the Medici Venus; from Antwerp, three Rubenses; from Venice, Titians

James Gillray symbolized the Peace of Amiens in 1802 with a kiss bestowed by a courtly Napoleon upon a robust Britannia. The sword by which Napoleon had conquered the Continent and the trident with which Britannia ruled the waves were amicably laid aside. But the peace was to be only a brief respite; after little more than 14 months the sword and trident were taken up again, and Gillray was drawing an arrogant "Little Boney" instead of a dashing diplomat.

and Tintorettos; and hundreds of other paintings from smaller cities.

The display was not to be missed. At least half a dozen Academicians made the journey from London, and Turner, predictably, was one of them. His "Studies in the Louvre" sketchbook, which includes 30 pages of notes and comment, reflects the enthusiasm of an explorer on fertile new ground. He was by no means overawed, however. He thought Rembrandt's *Susannah* "miserably drawn and poor in expression," a Rubens work "one continual glare of colour and absurdities." Color engrossed him above all. The pigments preferred by the masters and the ways in which they were deployed inspired detailed notes for future reference. Titian was decidedly Turner's favorite, supreme in "historical" as well as "natural" colors. The picture known as *Titian and His Mistress* evoked special praise on this score. "The Bosom of his Mistress," Turner wrote, "is a piece of Nature—in her happiest moments."

This was Turner in a rare mood of buoyancy. Leaving home and seeing new lands brought a sense of release. His very first glimpse of France had prompted an uncharacteristic caper. When the packet from Dover had to wait off Calais in choppy seas, he and a few daring spirits went ashore in a small boat, which nearly capsized. The escapade only fired his energies. When the packet finally docked, Turner was there on the jetty, busily sketching the waves breaking against it and the local fishermen preparing to cast off. The next year's Academy exhibition would show the result: the brilliant *Calais Pier (pages 66-67).*

Normally a loner, Turner welcomed company on his Continental venture. His main objective besides the Louvre was the Alps, which had lured him ever since he had copied them from John Robert Cozens' watercolors. In Paris he and some fellow travelers pooled funds, bought a cabriolet and set out for Lyons and Geneva. The tour took about three months and covered some of Europe's most vaunted natural wonders: Mont Blanc, the Alpine passes of St. Bernard and St. Gotthard, the spectacular 80-foot fall of the Rhine at Schaffhausen. Turner brought back some 400 drawings, a mine of ideas for the future.

Neither he nor his art would ever be the same. Personally, he was now more a man of the world, able to discuss the acidity of French and Swiss wines, the indolence of innkeepers and the need to "make bargains for everything, everywhere." Professionally, he had discovered a new face of nature, awesome, overpowering, diminishing man by its majesty. It left a lasting imprint. He would not love England's quieter scenery the less, but henceforth he would constantly be trying, in Ruskin's words, "to reconcile old fondnesses and new sublimities."

Turner was never more in tune with his times than during this first foreign foray. The spirit of Romanticism was on the rise; a zest for adventure and a boundless curiosity were its hallmarks. But simply to acquire knowledge was not enough. One had to react to it, personally and intensely. As opposed to the cool detachment of 18th Century Reason, 19th Century Romanticism gloried in involvement.

Eager to understand his world, the Romantic turned to nature. The merest leaf or the highest peak could unleash the imagination and evoke a variety of emotions. His favorite emotion was exaltation; his favorite

While the Peace of Amiens lasted, thousands of Englishmen, Turner among them, hastened to visit Paris. There they were dazzled by a vast display of precious art expropriated from the domains Napoleon had conquered. Curators like the one depicted here catalogued the treasures of Italy, Holland and Egypt, which overflowed the basement of the Louvre (officially renamed the Musée Napoléon). In 1815, after Napoleon's defeat at Waterloo, much of the plunder was retrieved from France by its original owners.

word, applied to whatever aroused this feeling, was "sublime." Above all, he experienced the sublime in the presence of nature at its most formidable. A raging sea or a towering mountain reminded him that man-made order was destructible. The thought was tinged with fear—and joy. Temperamentally, as one historian of the era has noted, the Romantic was a lawbreaker. As between civilization, with its restraints, and nature, untamed, he preferred nature. In politics he tended to be a supporter of revolution and reform; in creative endeavor an experimenter, probing beyond the limits of the status quo.

Expectably, the harbingers of the Romantic movement were poets. At the time Turner returned from France, literary London was astir over Wordsworth's *Lyrical Ballads,* which abandoned the measured formality of 18th Century Neoclassical verse and, in language even the common man could grasp, flaunted a frank intimacy of feeling. The "meddling intellect," Wordsworth argued in the preface, should be ignored; one should rely on one's senses for an awareness of the world.

The new mood was for Turner simply an affirmation. He was predisposed to the Romantic way both by instinct and experience. His journey through the Alps was in itself the quintessential Romantic gesture, for it was widely agreed that no place was more intoxicating to the senses. The drawings he brought back of mountain torrents and precipices, ice caps and rock masses showed a sure eye for sublime subject matter. Yet several years were to pass before Turner produced a full-blown Romantic painting. Though he shared many traits with the Romantics, impetuosity was not one of them. As always, he preferred to let his new ideas simmer before they took shape.

At this point he seemed more intent on proving to his fellow Academicians that they had not erred in admitting him to their midst. An astonishing versatility marked his entries in the 1803 exhibition. The biggest surprise was a *Holy Family,* a theme rare for Turner, executed in the manner of Titian. An idyllic landscape with figures, *Festival upon the Opening of the Vintage at Macon,* conjured up Claude. In *Châteaux de St. Michael, Bonneville, Savoy* he presented a scene of classical stillness reminiscent of Poussin. This virtuoso emulation of three very different masters did not satisfy Turner, however. A fourth exhibit was *Calais Pier,* a reminder of his special gift for sea pieces. But it differed from those which had won him earlier acclaim. With its still lifes of fish, its vignettes of a quarrelsome fishwife and a fisherman brandishing a bottle, it revealed yet another Turner talent, a flair for genre.

As at the previous year's show. Turner's work was much talked about. But this time the talk was a bit more controversial, a bit less complimentary. He had his defenders, including the genial Thomas Lawrence, and even some grudging praise from his detractors. No one could fault his patent respect for the masters, the merit of his themes, his general expertise. What riled people was his execution.

A Turner painting, they felt, never looked quite finished. The forms were not at all well defined, and whole sections of the picture were indistinct; one had to work at figuring out his intent. Closer scrutiny just added insult to injury. Turner's paint almost lunged out at the viewer, instead of being smoothly finished as academic tradition dictated; he seemed to have laid it on with a kind of brute relish, and then further hacked it up with his palette knife. There was also the annoyance of his colors. Not only were they applied in distracting blobs and dabs, but they were rather arbitrarily chosen. Everyone knew, for example, that the sea ought to be painted blue-green, yet in *Calais Pier* it appeared chalky white. In general Turner's colors seemed too bright, defying the customary dark tones. Sir George Beaumont, with his brown-as-a-fiddle theory, saw this as almost a personal affront. He was to become Turner's arch-foe, denouncing his "vicious practice" far and wide.

Most disquieting of all to the traditionalists was Turner's allure for younger painters—Constable excepted. Not yet free of Beaumont's influence, Constable shared his mentor's dim view of Turner, but with his usual honesty felt obliged to report that he was a minority of one among his contemporaries at the Academy. Turner's boldness, especially in color, charmed them, and their own work was showing it. Watching these upstart "white painters" who dared to scorn the conventional blacks and browns, their elders knew where to place the blame. An item in the magazine *True Briton* reported: "A certain artist has so much debauched the taste of the young artists in this country by the empirical novelty of his style of painting that a humorous critic gave him the title of *over-Turner*."

Turner stood fast against the hubbub; in fact, his self-assurance skyrocketed. Other painters gasped at his steep new prices—400 guineas for *Festival at Macon* alone—and at his refusal to dicker. At Academy meetings he was no longer the respectful Turner of before. He even tangled with his friend Farington. By rotation, he had secured a seat on the governing council; presiding one day, he reprimanded Farington and two others for briefly leaving the room. Stung, Farington told him that his behavior was a "cause of complaint to the whole Academy."

A sudden access of ego was not enough to account for Turner's show of contentiousness. His personal affairs were hardly conducive to serenity. In 1804 his mother died in a private insane asylum, and Turner was now faced with the care of an aging father. Another burden was the secret of Sarah Danby, whom he apparently had little thought of marrying, even though their daughter Evelina had been born a few years earlier. Ardor had evidently given way to humdrum; possibly, too, Sarah was showing a less attractive side. At any rate, an apparently original poem in one of Turner's sketchbooks begins: "Love is like the raging Ocean/ Winds that sway its troubled motion/ Woman's temper will supply . . ."

But if Turner had become abrasive and unpredictable in his dealings with most of the world, his intimate friends saw another side. He spent several nights a week at the home of the watercolorist W. F. Wells. While they peacefully sketched by lamplight and Mrs. Wells sewed, the oldest girl, Clara, would read aloud from some "useful or entertaining book." Once, on a weekend at the Wells' country place in Kent, Turner was found by Clara romping on the sitting-room floor with several of the younger children. In a letter written long afterward, she recalled, "No one would have imagined under that rough and cold ex-

This 1846 cartoon, showing Turner with a mop and a bucket of paint, reflects the derision his later painting style elicited from much of the public and some of his fellow artists. He painted with riotous colors and jabbed at his canvases with short, stubby brushes, end-on. One Varnishing Day a crowd of Turner's colleagues watched him manipulate his palette knife across the surface of his canvas, spreading a lump of unidentified stuff. An observer asked, "What's that he's plastering his picture with?" To which a painter who knew Turner replied, "I should be sorry to be the man to ask him!"

terior, how very strong were the affections which lay hidden beneath."

In previous years the Academy itself would have offered Turner the congeniality he sought, but in 1804 it, too, had its problems. A struggle for power within the membership had led to factionalism, which in turn brought interference by the King. As the Academy's august sponsor, George III, had always had this prerogative, but had seldom used it. He now began to dabble in Academy business, a peril all the harder to endure because of his odd whims and increasingly rare periods of lucidity. He had a bias against anyone he deemed "democratical." This blanket indictment covered a range of subversiveness, from Benjamin West's admiration of Napoleon to another painter's reported remark 10 years earlier, when Marie Antoinette was executed, that "the guillotine might well be employed upon some more crowned heads." When the author of this sentiment was elected the Academy's Keeper (administrator of the Academy school), George summarily vetoed him.

The intramural bickering and the King's meddling seemed to diminish the Academy and make its image less imposing. Turner decided that two showcases were better than one. In 1804 he opened his own gallery on the first floor of his Harley Street lodgings. It was one big, long room, about 20 by 70 feet, but he soon had it so crammed with pictures that it reminded one visitor of a "green stall [vegetable stand], rank, crude and disordered." Still, the gallery drew crowds.

Among the works on display was *The Shipwreck*, Turner's first major essay in Romanticism. The theme was of vital interest to a seafaring people—some 5,000 Englishmen perished in maritime disasters every year —and it was also high in the Romantics' catalogue of sublime horrors, the epitome of man's helplessness against nature. The painting was Turner's most powerful yet, linking sea, sky and victims in a triumph of turbulence incarnate. This time there was little carping at his wild ways; style and subject meshed perfectly. A prompt success, *The Shipwreck* became his first oil to be reproduced and sold as an engraving.

P reoccupied with his gallery, Turner did not submit any pictures to the Academy exhibition of 1805, breaking an annual habit that had begun with his debut in 1790. He was to resume it the very next year; still, he had proved to himself that the Academy was not necessarily the be-all and end-all for a painter. Several events of 1805 suggest he was not alone in this view. One was the founding of the British Institution, whose goal was "promoting the Fine Arts in the United Kingdom." Sponsored by a group of connoisseurs, it proposed to hold annual exhibitions of both old masters and current English works, and its aim to "excite the . . . exertion of younger artists" seemed to be a hint that the Academy was falling down on its job. Another challenge to the Academy's dominance was the first showing in 1805 of the new Society of Painters in Water-colours, formed in protest at the Academy's cavalier treatment of their medium: too often their entries had been hung in the glare of windows or consigned to a small, dark room. Seething over the slight, a score of watercolorists had struck out on their own, with astonishing success—their seven-week exhibition garnered a total of 12,000 paid admissions, and large sales as well.

A sudden glorious turn in the war made all the art world's churnings seem pallid. A strange but never-to-be-forgotten name leaped into the news: Trafalgar. Off this small cape in southwest Spain, on October 21, 1805, an English fleet under Admiral Nelson smashed a combined French-Spanish fleet under Admiral Villeneuve and in one bloody afternoon destroyed Napoleon's naval power.

Napoleon, now self-crowned Emperor of France, had brought on this disaster by a rare strategic blunder. Since the demise of the Peace of Amiens, his plans to dispatch the English had centered on an invasion of their island. He had marshaled 150,000 troops at the Channel port of Boulogne, and built 1,200 flat-bottomed boats; entirely confident, he had ordered a victory medal struck showing Hercules strangling a mermaid. Then the Emperor, on reflection, decided the Channel should be swept clean of English vessels before the invasion proceeded. He directed his navy to entice them out. It was in the ensuing hide-and-seek game, played across the Atlantic and back, that Nelson cornered the foe at Trafalgar.

The price was a hero's death. In the hour of triumph, Nelson, on the quarterdeck of his flagship *Victory*, took a musket ball through the lungs and spine. Two months later the *Victory* brought his body home, preserved upright in a barrel of rum. National mourning was mingled with gratitude. Ideas for commemorative gestures abounded, and Turner's was among the first. Evidently only hours after Nelson's body was taken off, Turner boarded the *Victory*, interviewed the crew and made sketches of uniforms and the ship. *The Battle of Trafalgar as Seen from the Mizen Starboard Shrouds of the Victory (page 65)* was unveiled at his gallery the next spring. The sea does not appear at all; the painting focuses instead on a confrontation of great ships, seen at close hand. The excitement of battle throbs everywhere, except in one pool of poignant quiet where Nelson lies in the arms of his men.

A stalemate followed Trafalgar. England could not be driven from the sea, nor Napoleon from the Continent. A new strategy was needed, and the Emperor found it in economics. His so-called Continental System, set up in 1806, forbade the countries under his control to buy any English goods. England countered with a blockade of Europe's ports and outgoing trade. All signs pointed to another long haul in the war, and the English settled back once again to their domestic affairs.

As the excitement over Trafalgar subsided, a new sensation took its place. An inquiry, discreetly labeled a Delicate Investigation, was ordered by George III to investigate charges that the Prince of Wales' estranged wife, Princess Caroline, had borne an illegitimate son and that she had carried on with several prominent men, including Thomas Lawrence, who had painted her portrait. Lawrence signed an affidavit that he had never been alone with Princess Caroline except in the afternoon, never in any place other than her drawing room, and never with the door closed beyond "the power of any person on the outside to open it." Caroline impishly allowed that she had committed adultery with only one man—"the husband of Mrs. Fitzherbert." The English guffawed and the Delicate Investigation ended.

An ornate "Trafalgar Cup," designed by the sculptor John Flaxman, was commissioned by the Patriotic Fund of Lloyd's insurance company to commemorate the Royal Navy's great victory over the French and Spanish fleets. At the center, Hercules is represented slaying the Hydra, an allegory for the British crushing French Imperialism. An overgrowth of victory laurels, the motto "Britons Strike Home" and a British lion complete the design. Flaxman executed monuments to famous people in similar style in Westminster Abbey and St. Paul's Cathedral, but he never found a patron to back his most heroic conception: a 230-foot-high statue of Britannia towering on a hillside in Greenwich.

The royal scandal left George III little time for Academy-watching. Its members breathed easier; congeniality once more prevailed. Turner, his gallery established, was again active in Academy affairs. His colleagues elected him Professor of Perspective, an honor that entailed an annual lecture series. He also undertook an artistic project unlike any he had tried before. His friend Wells, a man of lively ideas and a leader of the watercolorists' secession from the Academy, was a staunch believer in Turner's genius. He now urged Turner to publish a *Liber Studiorum*. Such a book of studies, intended to display the range of an artist's talents, had a precedent in Claude's *Liber Veritatis*. Wells proposed that Turner produce a series of drawings in various categories of landscape, then supervise a carefully selected engraver in reproducing them. The work could be done, and sold, piecemeal.

Dubious at first about taking on the problems of a publisher, Turner was won over when Wells argued that inferior engravings of his work might be published after his death and hurt his reputation. It seemed a little early to be worrying about post-mortems—Turner was just past 30—but the first installments of the *Liber Studiorum* appeared in 1807. By the time he dropped the project more than a decade later it comprised 71 engravings, a unique record of his diversity.

Perhaps spurred by his success at one innovation, Turner was experimenting in other directions as the first decade of the 19th Century neared its end. He had taken a modest house, shared by his father and tended by Hannah Danby, Sarah's niece, in outlying London, at Hammersmith on the Thames. The city's grime had not yet defiled the area; there were trees and quiet and a garden that ran down to the river's edge. There was also a summerhouse for a studio, but Turner had a better idea: he would paint outdoors, drifting along the Thames in a small boat. Indoor light and the confines of a room were "absurdities," he explained to a family friend—"A picture could be painted anywhere." Most of his colleagues would have disagreed; the outdoors was fine for sketching, but oil painting was studio work. In any case, Turner did not advertise his opinion. A century later, long after open-air painting had become routine, the storeroom "lumber" of the Turner Bequest yielded up almost a score of small oils executed on thin mahogany panels, beautifully rendering various places along the Thames as viewed from the river itself.

If Turner's contemporaries knew nothing of his open-air heresy, they had evidence of other disturbing trends in two paintings he exhibited at the Academy in 1807 and 1810. *Sun Rising through Vapour (page 68)* was ostensibly a picture of fishermen cleaning and selling fish; in fact, it was a celebration of color and light as entities in themselves, which persistently distracted the viewer from the "story." *Cottage Destroyed by an Avalanche* was supposedly set in the Alps, but the scene was maddeningly unidentifiable; its forms were so simplified—almost abstract—that it seemed more a flight of the imagination, an essay on nature's violence anywhere. Turner was playing havoc with artistic canon, and there was more to come in the next decade.

Constable, too, was at a turning point in his art. For him most of the

When Princess Caroline sat for the portraitist Thomas Lawrence in 1804, the result of the session was not only the painting above but a juicy scandal as well. Four witnesses testified during a subsequent "Delicate Investigation" that the Princess had made herself "familiar" with the artist. The investigators cleared Caroline of adultery, but censured her for her behavior toward Lawrence and two other men and for being "incautiously witty," particularly in discussing her husband, the Prince. The Princess' indiscretion cost her the friendship and protection of her only friend in the Royal family, old King George.

decade had passed in trying to stay afloat. The truthful landscapes he preferred to paint apparently were unpalatable to the public. What little he earned came from copying family portraits and Reynolds' paintings in the collection of a wealthy Suffolk peer, Lord Dysart, and from two altarpieces he painted for small churches near East Bergholt.

To make matters worse, people were always meddling in Constable's art. Lord Dysart's brother-in-law, for example, fascinated with his 13-year-old ward's eyes, was all for Constable's painting a miniature of one of them to decorate a shirtpin. Through Beaumont, Constable met Wordsworth; the poet grandly offered to suggest subjects for him. But Constable bore all with good grace, and in his private hours pursued his objective of truth in art. Two paintings that particularly signaled his emergence as a wholly original artist, *Malvern Hall* and *Shipping on the Orwell*, are unabashedly naturalistic and joyously rendered; the colors are bright, the brushwork lively, the handling relaxed.

In Constable's new creativity money seemed secondary. His mother agreed. In 1810, at a time when Turner was totting up his stockholdings and finding that they came to more than £7,200, a letter from Ann Constable to her son spoke slightingly of "the love of filthy lucre." In any event, Constable now had a greater passion to enjoy. He had fallen in love with a dark-eyed young lady whom he had known as a child, and who was now a lissome 22: Maria Bicknell, the granddaughter of the rector of East Bergholt.

The man who was to become the Duke of Wellington, Arthur Wellesley, was 39 when he took command of an English army of 9,000 men and embarked for the Iberian Peninsula to challenge Napoleon's legions. Just before Wellesley left, in 1808, London artist Richard Cosway painted this locket-sized miniature portrait. Wellesley's success against the French in Spain, and later at Waterloo, made him England's greatest soldier-hero.

It was also in 1810 that George III celebrated the 50th year of his reign. Many of his subjects were newly prosperous; even the war was going better. Having finally decided that Napoleon could only be beaten on land and by English troops, the king's ministers had sent an expeditionary force to the Iberian Peninsula. Its commander was Sir Arthur Wellesley, soon to be Duke of Wellington, a ramrod of a man, hardnosed, crotchety and certain of his prowess. He was having his troubles, to be sure, some of them with his aristocratic officers. They had to be ordered not to use umbrellas against the battlefield sun, and not to overstay their 48-hour leaves in Lisbon. (This, the general declared, was "as long as any reasonable man can wish to stay in bed with some woman.") But such problems were minor. What counted was that an English army had secured a Continental foothold, and stood ready to engage the French wherever they appeared.

Affairs of state, so far as George III was able to discern them dimly, were in relative order. But his family was something else again. After the Delicate Investigation into Caroline's affairs had come a Parliamentary inquiry into allegations that the King's second son, the Duke of York, had peddled Army commissions under the malign influence of his inamorata, a common tart. York was no sooner exonerated than George's fifth son, the Duke of Cumberland, was suspected of killing his valet in a fit of rage. The King's only comforts were his daughters, especially his pet and youngest child, Amelia. Then, in November of 1810, Amelia suddenly died. The King's mind snapped, and three months later the firstborn to whom he had never become reconciled, the 49-year-old Prince of Wales, was sworn in as Regent of the Realm.

A Bold Beginning

Turner was schooled in traditional ways, but in the variety and boldness of his early painting he often shocked the English art establishment. Like many another young artist, he earned his living copying watercolors and coloring engravers' prints while learning technical skills. He advanced so rapidly however, that he was named an associate member of the Royal Academy of Arts when he was only 24 years old; three years later he was made a full academician, an honor coveted by men twice his age. During this time he attained popularity with English landscapes and seascapes, works skillfully done but not notable for testing the imagination of the viewer. He also established a reputation among his peers and critics by painting what serious English artists customarily painted —Bible stories and classical mythology in the manner of earlier masters, as well as scenes from English history past and present *(right)*.

Although few in the art world ever doubted his talent, the direction of Turner's painting gradually made many uncomfortable. He seemed to attack the very concept of form even while painting traditional scenes; he sanctified light and color as more than mere pictorial elements, often allowing them to dominate his subject. This radical view dismayed many of his colleagues and critics, and some of his early canvases went unsold. But Turner kept at his work until the hints suggested in his early paintings matured into the masterpieces of his later years.

In the narrative style typical of his early work, Turner re-created the tragic death of the British hero Lord Nelson at the moment his ships were defeating Napoleon's fleet at Trafalgar in 1805. The scene focuses sharply on Nelson lying in the arms of his men aboard his flagship *Victory*—Turner has rendered even the distant flags and rigging in precise detail to heighten the overall dramatic effect.

The Battle of Trafalgar as Seen from the Mizen Starboard Shrouds of the Victory, 1806-1808

Turner's lifelong passion for the sea is revealed in *Calais Pier (left)*, a realistic drama of the restless ocean and the men who dare to battle it. As he did with many of his paintings, Turner based this one on a personal experience. When he was crossing the Channel on his way to Paris in 1802, a storm prevented the landing of his packet. Turner managed to get ashore in a small boat and stood on the pier sketching the progress of the packet fighting its way in.

Turner's penchant for breaking tradition is evident here. Where many artists would have portrayed even a stormy sea as dark green or blue, he made the waves peak and swell in a white froth of fury. In this tumult, the struggling packet tosses against the darkness of the clouds; from the pier French fishermen, watched by their families, set out stoically into the storm. Uniting the foreground action with the background, the pier tapers sharply, leading the viewer's eye to the horizon, a razor-thin line of white; in the sky, livid storm clouds are broken by a patch of clear blue.

Calais Pier, with French Poissards Preparing for Sea: An English Packet Arriving, exhibited 1803

Sun Rising through Vapour, Fishermen Cleaning and Selling Fish, exhibited 1807

The tranquillity of nature inspired Turner as deeply as its violence. The early works shown here capture two quieter moments, one at the shore, the other inland. *Sun Rising through Vapour (above)* radiates the idle charms of a morning in a seaside town after a night of fishing. The boats are snug in the harbor; some of the fishermen chat over drinks, while others clean their catch. The light is important to the mood: the peaceful glow of the sun's rays suffuses the picture with warmth.

When *Frosty Morning (above, right)* was exhibited in 1813, many British critics hailed it as Turner's finest work. Even the Reverend John Fisher, an old friend of

Frosty Morning, exhibited 1813

the painter John Constable, preferred the Turner work to the Constable landscape that hung at the same exhibition. Slightly embarrassed at his admission, Fisher wrote to Constable, "Don't repine . . . You are a great man, like Bonaparte, and are only to be beaten by a frost." (Napoleon had recently been forced to retreat from Russia because of the brutally cold winter.)

Turner based this painting on a rural tableau he had seen from his coach while traveling in Yorkshire. The scene is exquisitely simple, but once again Turner added his own unexpected and original touch, lightening the dark foreground with sparkling hoarfrost.

Crossing the Brook, exhibited

Pilate Washing His Hands, exhibited 1830

In his early work, Turner was clearly under the influence of older masters. His landscapes owed much to the 17th Century French painter Claude, whose compositions were subtly balanced, all the elements fitting together with formal precision. Turner appreciated these virtues, as can be seen in *Crossing the Brook (left)*, a scene inspired by the River Tamar in Devon. Like Claude, Turner has imbued his painting with a romantic haze. But this is no copy of Claude;

Turner has exaggerated the framework of the trees, creating an imbalance by heightening those at the left until they gush like spumes of water from a fountain.

By contrast, *Pilate Washing His Hands (above)*, in which the figures are small in scale, yet dominate the picture, is done in a manner reminiscent of Rembrandt. The palette is earth-toned and the lighting diffuse. Turner's colors are brighter, however, his lighter tones foretelling the luminous hues of his later work.

Two dramatic components of Turner's later art are clearly foretold in *Hannibal Crossing the Alps (above)* and *Ulysses Deriding Polyphemus (following pages)*. By custom, painters arranged such historical and mythological scenes in horizontal and vertical planes that yielded a foreground, middleground and background. To achieve the dramatic effect he wanted in *Hannibal*, however, Turner substituted the circular swirl of a storm for the traditional verticals and horizontals. The soldiers, interrupted in their plundering of a mountain village by the storm, cringe beneath its exaggerated vortex. Here Turner has repeated one of his

Snowstorm: Hannibal and His Army Crossing the Alps, exhibited 1812

favorite themes—men humbled by nature's titanic force.

The setting of *Ulysses* shows Turner's continuing absorption with the ability of light and color to convey emotion. Here he tells the story of the escape of Ulysses and his men from the Cyclops Polyphemus, who had kept them imprisoned in a cave. After blinding the Cyclops, the triumphant Ulysses and his men set sail in a blaze of glory, the glowing colors of the sun and sky heralding their freedom. This exuberance of color horrified many of Turner's contemporaries, accustomed as they were to the somber hues of the old masters, but it provided a brilliant forecast of the work to come.

Ulysses Deriding Polyphemus, exhibited 1829

IV

A Royal
Pacesetter

After two decades of waiting in the wings, England's new Prince Regent wanted to celebrate his accession in style. Whatever his faults—and even friends agreed "Prinney" had many—his sense of occasion was matchless. The grand ball and banquet he announced for June 19, 1811, promised to be the most lavish in memory. For many of the 2,000 invited guests this was to be their first look inside London's finest palace, Carlton House, which had been the Prince's own establishment since his coming-of-age in 1783. Time and again he had renovated and redecorated it, incessantly changing its furniture and filling it with objets d'art at a cost that caused both parental and Parliamentary anguish. A scene sometimes of debauch, sometimes of musicales and scholarly discussion, Carlton House was a fitting backdrop for its complex master—dissolute, cultivated, irrepressible and irresponsible.

As a host that evening he literally shone. Having just appointed himself a field marshal, he wore a uniform he had designed to suit the rank—scarlet awash in gold lace. On his chest was the diamond star of the Order of the Garter; jewels in his sword hilt and in his plumed wig added to the dazzle. If his complexion seemed uncommonly close to his coat color, his ample figure was still able to execute the deepest of bows, one of his special conceits.

With the raptness of sightseers the guests moved about, inspecting the great hall with its columns of porphyry, the double staircase with its bronze Atlas upholding the world, the blue velvet anteroom hung with Dutch masters, the Chinese drawing room all in yellow silk. As absorbing as the décor were the whispers about those present and those not. Conspicuously absent were the host's two wives. He had once vowed that he would "rather see toads and vipers crawling over my victuals" than sit at the same table with Princess Caroline. Mrs. Fitzherbert had declined to come when informed that she would not, as in previous years, grace the Regent's side. His current favorite, the Marchioness of Hertford, however, was much in evidence.

Gossip would thrive for months on these tidbits, and on the evening's climax. At 2:30 A.M. supper was served in the conservatory,

Connoisseur and libertine, patron of the arts and friend of dandies, the Prince of Wales commenced his glittering Regency in 1811 less qualified in matters of state than in matters of style. This portrait of him reflects perfectly the modish spirit of his era.

Sir Thomas Lawrence: *George IV as Prince Regent,* 1815

built to resemble a Gothic nave. To accommodate the overflow, the 200-foot-long main table branched out into the adjoining gardens. Wherever they were seated, guests could glimpse the spectacular centerpiece the Prince had devised: a fountain in the form of a miniature temple. Flowing from it in a trough the length of the table, six inches above the silver service, was a stream of water banked with moss and flowers and filled with fish. Some of these, ingrates noted, were dead or dying; still, appetites rallied to tackle a repast of more than a hundred dishes, washed down by champagne. Coiffures wilted and uniforms grew soggy in the heat, but enough energy remained for dancing until dawn.

As details of the gala became known, 19-year-old Percy Bysshe Shelley sent a bristling letter to a friend. "What think you," he wrote, "of the bubbling *brooks* and *mossy banks* at Carlton House . . . ? It is said that this entertainment will cost £120,000. Nor will it be the last bauble which the nation must buy for this overgrown bantling [brat] of Regency." These were strong words, but Shelley passionately meant them. Like another well-born young poet, Lord Byron, he was soon to emerge as one of a crop of new talents incensed at the inequities in English life. Many echoed their outrage, and the Regent personified it.

The English were generally edgy. The war was nearing its 20th year and no end was in sight, despite some success by Wellington's army against the French forces in Spain. True, Napoleon had pulled back his best troops for a new campaign against Russia, but the thought that he might lose it was preposterous. Adding to London's gloom was the prospect of war with the United States. In an effort to curb all trade with France, the English had taken to stopping American ships enroute to and from the Continent and seizing sailors they claimed were English. The Yankees were boiling, and bent on a collision course that was to result in the War of 1812.

Domestic woes also abounded. Bad harvests throughout England and the uncertainty of grain imports had sent wheat prices sky-high. Many of the poor were starving. Work was hard to come by. Industrialism, replacing men with machines, seemed less a cornucopia than a curse. In the manufacturing town of Nottingham, a youth named Ned Ludd smashed some machinery in anger and thereby launched a movement to smash it by design. As the Luddites rampaged through the mills of the Midlands, the government decreed machine-breaking a capital offense. Nottingham responded with riots. In the House of Lords, Byron reported on a visit to the area. "Never in the most oppressed provinces of Turkey," he declared, "did I behold such squalor as I have seen in the very heart of a Christian country."

Byron did not need to place the blame. Sooner or later England's every trouble was laid at the Regent's door. Hoping to be loved, he was destined to be loathed. Few of his frailties escaped censure. The normally gentle essayist Charles Lamb jibed at his expanding girth in an ode to the "Prince of W(h)ales." The satirist Peter Pindar mocked at his penchant for mature women in a barnyard analogy that ended: "Among the whole, not one in ten/Could please him like a tough old Hen." Most devastating was an article by the journalist Leigh Hunt on

England's infamous "press gangs," which sometimes brutally recruited Yankee mariners on shore leave, often simply clubbed men down and dragged them off to "join" the Royal Navy and sail against Napoleon. Englishmen were not safe either; drunks and derelicts were rounded up, tradesmen were snatched from their shops, and occasionally a strolling gentleman was carried off. In the country, the painter John Constable's father reported that press gangs had even shanghaied some of the local bargemen who worked for him on the River Stour's canals.

the Regent's 50th birthday. The savagery of the attack was to land the author in jail, but many shared his view of his target: ". . . a libertine over head and ears in debt and disgrace, a despiser of domestic ties, the companion of gamblers and demireps, a man who has just closed half a century without one single claim on the gratitude of his country or the respect of posterity."

One sector of the nation saw the Regent otherwise. The worlds of art, science and scholarship adored him. His interest in these fields was genuine. For all his frivolity, his education had been rigorous. He had studied Greek and Latin and the classics, and was fluent in French, German and Italian. Alexander Cozens had taught him to draw. He played the cello, and enjoyed string quartets.

Creative people in any field stirred his admiration and support. Humphrey Davy, who discovered chlorine and nitrous oxide—laughing gas— and who invented the safety lamp, was knighted, much to his own surprise; the honor, he noted, "has not often been bestowed on scientific men." The same distinction was to go to the most popular author of the day, Walter Scott, along with the pleasure of "snug little dinners," as the Regent described them, at Carlton House. Jane Austen, in London to nurse her sick brother, was tracked down, invited to inspect the Regent's extensive library, and flattered to learn that he kept a set of her sedate novels of country life in each of his residences.

Men and women of attainment were charmed by the Regent's personal touch, and by the signs that he was more than a mere dabbler. However blind to his country's social and economic ills, he was determined to improve its cultural and intellectual life. To this end there was no effort he would not foster, and often directly finance, from the endowment of readerships at Oxford to the purchase of ancient Roman papyrus scrolls unearthed in the digs at Herculaneum.

Among those who could count on his devotion were, of course, the painters. His own collection, heavy in 17th Century Dutch, Flemish and French works, reflected a Continental taste. But he had long since lent his patronage to native talents as well, starting with Reynolds and Gainsborough. Thomas Lawrence, despite his involvement as one of Princess Caroline's alleged lovers, was now the Regent's favorite. Scottish-born David Wilkie, a painter of genre, also caught his fancy. His purchase of Wilkie's *Penny Wedding* and *Blind Man's Buff* helped launch a vogue for sentimental themes that lasted through the Victorian era.

Both Lawrence and Wilkie were eventually knighted, and their Royal Academy colleagues also stood to benefit. Where George III had meddled in Academy politics, his son spurred its pursuit of excellence. He was happy to oblige when its officials asked for the loan of the Raphael cartoons in the royal collection and for casts of antique statues to use for teaching. On his calendar there was almost always room for the opening of the Academy's annual exhibition and the ensuing dinner. After the first dinner he attended on becoming Regent, he presented the Academy with a specially commissioned bronze lamp to hang from the ceiling of the banquet hall. The gesture was not perfunctory. He had noticed, he explained, that the candles on the table cast a glare on the paintings on the walls. Such a prince, it was agreed, could only be loved.

Ironically, England's greatest patron of the arts overlooked its greatest landscape painters. No knighthood awaited Turner or Constable. Through his beloved Maria's father, who was one of the Regent's solicitors, Constable was presented to His Royal Highness but made no known impression. Turner fared no better, although he briefly had cause for hope of royal favor. At the same Academy dinner that produced the gift of the lamp, the Regent made a short speech praising the paintings on exhibit, including "landscapes which Claude would have admired." In retrospect, this offers a clue to his neglect of Turner and Constable; their innovations were not likely to appeal to someone who thought Claude the ultimate in landscape mastery. But at the time, the remark was thought to have been aimed at a Turner entry executed in the Claude manner, *Mercury and Herse*, and talk spread that the Regent intended to buy the painting. The rumor was false and Turner was acutely embarrassed by it; even worse, until the story petered out he was unable to entertain authentic offers for the work.

Undoubtedly Turner would have relished princely patronage. But he was as sensible to its pitfalls as to its pleasures. He recorded his thoughts on the subject, and on painting in general, in penciled notes in the margins of two books on painting he owned. A patron, he observed, could be a "fetter upon genius," a hindrance to a painter who dared to think for himself; even at the cost of beggary one had to resist humbly deferring to a patron's opinions. "This stand is mine," Turner wrote, "and shall remain my own." He enumerated the means by which he felt greatness in art was—and was not—achieved. Not patrons, influential relatives nor even perseverance and industry could push an artist to the heights. The key, rather, was "an innate power that enforces, that inspires, and without which labor would be . . . a vain drudgery."

Turner had this power and knew it; he seemed able to command it at will. His attitude toward his art was almost imperious; he painted whatever and however he chose. Other artists, while resigned to this maverick in their midst, still found his unpredictability maddening. No sooner had they decided that Turner had settled down than he would stun them with some fresh outrage.

Three paintings he produced during this period reminded his audience of his bewildering versatility. In *Crossing the Brook (page 70)* he once again emulated Claude. He borrowed the Frenchman's harmony of composition and some of his celebrated devices—a tall tree in the foreground, a viaduct in the distant haze—and built them into an English landscape. The two young girls on either side of the brook (who may have been his daughters by Sarah Danby, Evelina and Georgiana) have the gentle mien of Claude's people.

In contrast to this study in timeless serenity, *Frosty Morning (page 69)* captured a single bleak moment Turner had glimpsed from a coach in Yorkshire. In a barren field stand a man with a hunting rifle and a girl holding a rabbit. Precisely what has caught their attention is a question viewers of the painting have never resolved. It may be a fencing and ditching operation; it may be a burial. In any case, all is as naturalistic as photographic journalism. No camera, however, would surpass Turner's rendition of the hoarfrost of a country morning.

In these two works Turner skillfully mingled the old and new. There was nothing in the general effect of either work to ruffle traditionalists, yet there were novelties enough to interest the venturesome. *Crossing the Brook* was in a much lighter color key than Claude would have used. *Frosty Morning* defied the venerable custom of a dark foreground and brought the light boldly front and center through the shimmer of frost-covered earth. Both paintings flouted two widely accepted conventions of landscape: they lacked classical or historical allusions, and they made no pretense at topographical precision. Instead, in a portentous development for later landscape art, the emphasis was on the expression of a mood.

Such innovations sat well with Turner's contemporaries because they were unobtrusive. But in the third masterpiece Turner thrust caution aside; that it was produced by the same hand was hard to believe. About all that remained of tradition was the painting's theme, as expressed in the title—*Snowstorm: Hannibal and His Army Crossing the Alps (pages 72-73)*.

Hannibal shattered the customary rules that called for a picture to be composed in horizontals and verticals, with diagonals to convey a sense of movement. For the kind of violent action Turner had in mind that formula was too tame. Instead, he made his painting a mass of curving forms—round, oval, elliptical—that interact to create the effect of a giant vortex. Overwhelmingly predominant among these forms is the snowstorm, filling the bowl of the mountain pass. The Carthaginian soldiers, stopped short in the act of pillaging by the ferocity of the storm, seem pygmies by comparison; the strength of man crumbles before the strength of nature.

In both style and symbolism *Hannibal* presaged Turner's most powerful works, his mystical hymns to nature's primacy. These works were a long time coming; as always, he was willing to let an idea mature slowly. The genesis of *Hannibal* itself was an example. Turner had attracted a steady patron quite unlike the irksome type he had damned in his private notes. Sir Walter Fawkes admired Turner without cavil, and often asked him to his estate, Farnley Hall, to fish and shoot grouse and sketch. Once a furious storm kept Turner indoors. Watching from a window, he made notes of its color and form on the back of a letter. Fawkes' son, Hawksworth, recalled: "He was absorbed—he was entranced. There was the storm rolling and sweeping and shafting out its lightning over the Yorkshire hills. Presently the storm passed and he finished. 'There! Hawkey,' he said, 'in two years you will see this again, and call it Hannibal crossing the Alps.' "

For those who viewed the finished work at the Academy in 1812 an extra surprise was in store: Turner emerged in the role of poet as well as painter. Under their listings in the exhibition catalogue, artists were allowed to insert lines of prose or verse to identify any historical figures in a painting, or simply to credit its source of inspiration. Up to now Turner had drawn on such classics as Milton's *Paradise Lost* and

James Thomson's *The Seasons;* indeed, Thomson's brilliant imagery would serve Turner recurrently as a mine of ideas. But with *Hannibal* he offered some verse of his own, an 11-line extract from an opus he called *Fallacies of Hope.*

This work was not his only poetic effort—a sketchbook filled with poetry came to light after his death—but it was the most curious. So far as is known no one ever saw it in completed or even cohesive form, although Turner was still offering fragments of it 40 years later. The suspicion was strong that he wrote *Fallacies of Hope* as he went along. Apart from the somber view of human destiny implied in the title, the poem's meaning defied easy understanding. Four of the lines that appeared with *Hannibal* suffice to indicate Turner's literary style: "Still the chief advanc'd,/Look'd on the sun with hope;—low, broad, and wan;/While the fierce archer of the downward year/Stains Italy's blanch'd barrier with storms." The poem was none too kindly received; one wit dismissed it as "all fallacy and very little hope."

Essentially, Turner seems to have been moved by a desire to elevate the status of landscape painting, to place it on a plane with the grandeur of noble poetry. Obviously, however, verbal communication was not his forte. This was evident also in the annual Academy lectures required of him as Professor of Perspective. Nervous about speaking in public, he managed to delay the lectures for three years. When he finally began them in 1811 his audiences, though charmed by the drawings and diagrams he had prepared to illustrate his points, were baffled by his cryptic mumblings. What emerged was his reverence for Claude and Reynolds; the radical notions brewing in his head went undisclosed.

Turner's agonies before a sea of faces were to be expected. For all the prestige he had acquired, poise still eluded him; he remained a very private person. The name he chose for a retreat he built in 1812 at Twickenham, on London's outskirts, was Solus Lodge. Although he later changed the name to Sandycombe Lodge, he had made it clear that his home was to be a fortress against intruders. Nearing 40, he was gaining fame as an eccentric. Middle age had not made him any more prepossessing: he had rough, weathered features and added poundage had turned his figure from merely short to squat. Nothing he wore fitted; colleagues joked that he haunted the "old clo" shops. He was widely considered a miser. Some thought him ungenerous even in matters of art. They resented his going off to sketch by himself when others were around, and his reluctance to show the results.

Occasionally Turner confounded the legend. A journalist friend, Cyrus Redding, reported that Turner had paid for the wine and food for a picnic and had proved himself to be "exceedingly agreeable." In June of 1813, Constable sat next to him at an Academy dinner and wrote Maria: "I was a good deal entertained with Turner . . . he is uncouth, but has a wonderful range of mind."

Constable's problems at the time were of a different order. For good or ill, Turner's art was at least talked about. Constable's met mostly with polite silence. Twice he had tried for an Academy Associateship and twice the selection committee had passed him over, once without a

As Professor of Perspective at the Royal Academy, Turner prepared nearly 200 large illustrations for his lectures. Among them was this print of *The Transfiguration* by Raphael, on which he superimposed lines analyzing the plan of the composition. In other illustrations, Turner diagrammed the play of moonlight on Trajan's column and showed the refraction of light passing through glass and water. He was a nervous speaker and delivered half his words with his back to the audience, interspersing his text with muttered directions to the attendant holding the illustrations. It was said that his visual aids were so interesting, however, that his lectures were enjoyed even by the Academy's old librarian, who was deaf.

single vote. His single-minded pursuit of truth in art seemed fruitless.

Still, he doggedly went on. During this period he was producing some of his most characteristic and appealing landscapes: *Dedham Vale: morning, Lock on the Stour,* and—painted entirely in the open air—*Boat-Building near Flatford Mill (page 123)*. In his recording of these peaceful scenes affection as well as artistry was at work. He bathed them not only in a wonderful harmony of light and atmosphere, but, it seemed, in an all-suffusing tenderness. His ardor spoke also in the vibrant energy of his brushwork. Carping critics found the effect unfinished; he did not care.

Another scene, away from Suffolk, was claiming Constable's interest: the pleasant cathedral town of Salisbury. He visited there as guest of its bishop, an old family friend whom he would one day eulogize as "my kind monitor for 25 years." To some His Lordship seemed stuffy; the Regent's hoydenish daughter, young Princess Charlotte, with whose moral guidance the bishop had been charged, had dubbed him "the great U.P." for the way he stressed the last syllable of "bishop." But Constable found him ever generous, ready to sit for his portrait and to suggest other commissions. His nephew, John Fisher, became the painter's closest friend. Salisbury was an inviting place to sketch. There were soft meadows and old trees and everywhere a sight of the looming cathedral spire. Constable first showed a view of Salisbury at the Academy in 1812, launching the magnificent series of sketches and oils of the cathedral with which his name would always be linked.

He might have produced more in these years, but love kept him in turmoil. His feeling for Maria was returned; but for a time, when he seemed overeager, her parents forbade him to call. He had to lurk about for snatched meetings in St. James's Park, or be satisfied with letter-writing. Actually the Bicknells liked him, but he had a formidable hurdle in Maria's rich and crusty Grandfather Rhudde. The Constables were prominent among Dr. Rhudde's parishioners at East Bergholt, yet their son, with his dubious vocation, seemed to the minister scarcely a match for Maria. He warned her family that if she pursued the romance he would disown her.

Constable's mother, aching for him, tried diplomacy. He had made her a watercolor she prized of the East Bergholt church. At her urging he made a copy and sent it to the rector in token of his esteem. It was acknowledged with stiff courtesy and a banknote in payment. As other deferential gestures failed, Constable moped and even occasionally took to his bed in his depression. Constable's mother besought him not to "pine away your prime," and suggested more diligent application to his art. Maria herself analyzed matters tersely. The key to their dilemma, she noted, was "that necessary article, Cash."

In a burst of renewed spirit, Constable took on all the portrait commissions he could muster. Although his fee was modest—15 guineas a head—he was able to write to Maria of a turn in the economic tide: "I am now leaving London for the only time in my life with pockets full of money. I am entirely free from debt." He sounded jubilant, but there was another triumph he longed for. He was aware that all his sales had been to friends concerned more for him than for his art. He yearned for some total stranger to admire his work on an exhibition wall and straightway decide to buy it. In 1814 his dream came true. Not one, but two strangers turned up to purchase landscapes. At last, he felt, he was on his way.

There was other cause for joy in 1814—joy that every Englishman could share. Early in April, bells pealed and bonfires blazed to signal the end of the 21-year war with France. Napoleon's second front against Russia had proved a total disaster. As his fortunes waned, England and its allies closed in. On April 12 Napoleon abdicated. The victors were unexpectedly magnanimous; they not only gave him a pension but allowed him to keep his title of Emperor and a tiny patch of his once vast realm, the Mediterranean island of Elba.

As Napoleon sailed for Elba, London braced for a colossal spree. A showman like the Regent could want no less. Building facades glowed with giant illuminated signs that read PEACE, UNANIMITY, THANKS BE TO GOD. The parks were laced with lanterns, and fireworks and special events were staged for the common people—a balloon ascent, and a mock battle by a toy navy on the lake in Hyde Park.

There were great personages to gape at as well: England's own military hero, Wellington; the exiled Louis XVIII, brother and successor of the beheaded Louis XVI, en route back to Paris to reclaim the Bourbon throne; and two visiting potentates, Czar Alexander of Russia and King Frederick William III of Prussia. For these imposing allies the Regent outdid himself in a round of balls and dinners, in a visit to Oxford for honorary degrees, and in a review of the fleet at Portsmouth—a scene Turner sketched and later painted. Even if the cheers were far louder for the foreigners than for him, the Regent was in his element. As the festivities ended in August, he had added reason for elation. Princess Caroline decided she had had enough of ostracism, and left for Europe. The thorn in his side was gone, he hoped, for good.

Gradually Napoleon faded from people's thoughts; when they talked of him it was to quip about the amount of "Elba-room" he had. Then, in March of 1815, he slipped back to France. With swelling support, he advanced on Paris. Louis XVIII fled. At the Congress of Vienna, convened to redraw the map of Europe, the diplomats' dickering halted. Some 70,000 English and Allied troops stood ready in the Low Countries at the French border. Napoleon's dream of renewed glory lasted a hundred days. It ended in a savage battle on June 18 in which he personally matched strategies with Wellington. The place of decision was a stretch of rolling Belgian farmland, around a village named Waterloo.

Soon afterward, aboard an English warship off Plymouth, the fallen dictator wrote the Regent asking for asylum in England: "I come, like Themistocles, to sit at the hearth of the British people." It was, the Regent conceded, "upon my word, a very proper letter," but approving the proposal would have annoyed the newly re-enthroned Louis XVIII. Napoleon's haven, it was decided, would be St. Helena, an island in the Atlantic reassuringly far from Europe.

"Hallelujah...that things are what they are," one of the Regent's brothers had written him, and he agreed. It was a relief to turn from matters of state to more gentlemanly diversions. In late 1815 he was keeping posted on the art news from Paris. Allied agents had converged to repossess the treasures Napoleon had wrested from their lands. Troops had to curb a surly crowd as foreign workmen climbed the Arc de Triomphe du Carrousel to remove the four bronze horses that had come from St. Mark's in Venice. Paris was stripped of a great many treasures, but there remained the splendor with which the city had been built up in the Napoleonic era. The Regent was inspired to do the same for London. Almost daily he pored over sketches with his favorite architect, John Nash. The ambitious master plan called for a broad, mile-long thoroughfare lined with stately buildings and covered colonnades—and named Regent Street—to extend in a sweeping curve from Carlton House to the site of an old royal hunting preserve. This terrain—named Regent's Park—was to be laid out with gardens, groves and villas. Ringing the park would be terraces of handsome residences and, behind them, streets of houses, working quarters and markets for less affluent Londoners.

Building began shortly after the war and was to continue, with some modification forced by lack of funds, for more than a decade. The concept of a "royal mile" and a "garden city" stamps Nash today as a pioneer townplanner. The Regent's role in initiating this and similar projects constitutes, in one historian's words, "the greatest contribution ever made by an English monarch to the enduring beauty of his country." Ironically, however, this effort by the Regent, intended for the public good, stirred the most violent public hostility. Popular opinion regarded these works as monstrously extravagant, and the Regent as indescribably callous. Indeed, the truth was that he could not have picked a worse time to spend money on city beautification.

With the peace half a million men were demobilized, only to join an army of unemployed created by the shutting down of factories whose war contracts had ended. England had emerged from the war supreme over the seas and with greater trading advantages than ever. But only a relative few were deriving the benefit. The division between them and the less fortunate was growing all the time as industrialism flourished, and the cleavage was dramatically sharpened by the Corn Laws of 1815. Parliament, controlled by Tory landowners with farming interests to protect, voted to ban the import of corn and other grains until domestic prices reached a specified high. The result was skyrocketing prices for grain and bread, and starvation for thousands of people both in the city and country. The crime rate rose all over England. The Luddites went on new rampages, bread riots flared in the cities, landowners' barns and hay ricks were set afire, and many of the hated new threshing machines were destroyed. Mass meetings demanded Parliamentary reform and equal representation. The furor reached a peak at St. Peter's Fields in Manchester, where mounted yeomen with sabers inflicted death and injury on a crowd of 60,000, gathered to hear a radical leader. Alarmed by the incident at "Peterloo"—bitingly renamed for Waterloo—Parliament voted to curb freedom of speech, press and assembly. The voic-

A star-crossed statue, this 11-foot-4-inch marble nude of Napoleon was commissioned by the Emperor himself from the Italian sculptor Antonio Canova. Although he apparently approved of its heroic, Neoclassical quality when it was delivered in 1811, he was said to have been offended that the small victory figure in the statue's right hand was turning her back on him as though to fly away. The Emperor's displeasure probably would have increased immeasurably had he known what would happen to the work after his fall. In 1816 France sold it to England, where it was deposited temporarily but ingloriously in the Duke of Richmond's outhouse until presented to Napoleon's conqueror, the Duke of Wellington, by the Regent. The statue ended up in a stairwell of Wellington's London house.

WELLINGTON MUSEUM, LONDON

es of dissent and the calls for reform were stilled—for about a decade.

Today, artists are often in the van of social protest. But Regency painters, with rare exceptions, either were or hoped to be part of polite society. People on this level recoiled at riots, even if some of them championed reform. Turner's beginnings suggest a natural sympathy for the plight of the poor, yet he had climbed far by his own bootstraps and perhaps expected the same of others. A clue to his thoughts may lie in his paintings of *Dido Building Carthage* and *The Destruction of Carthage*. In theme these works deal with the rise and fall of a great empire. Turner chose to show them successively in 1815 and 1817, when England itself was outwardly triumphant, internally troubled.

Of Constable's political views there is no doubt: he was a confirmed Tory, in the conservative tradition of most well-to-do country families. But generally, like Turner, Constable was too involved with his art to be much concerned with politics. And during the summer of 1816 he had even further cause to be preoccupied. In August he received a letter from his friend Fisher which he sent on to Maria. He was now 40, she 28. Fisher, recently ordained, was also 28, but he wrote to Constable with almost parental firmness. He mentioned a date when he would be in London, proclaimed his readiness to perform the marriage ceremony, and urged Constable to "get you to your lady, and instead of blundering out long sentences about the 'hymeneal altar,'" fix a wedding date. On October 2, with Fisher officiating, Constable and Maria were married at the church of St. Martin's-in-the-Fields. Success in his art became imperative.

To Turner success was becoming habitual. His paintings fetched as much as 550 guineas each. Another lucrative source of income had opened up in the booming market for illustrated books. Publishers were glad to pay him 25 guineas apiece for watercolors to be reproduced as engravings. Among the projects which engaged him were *Picturesque Views on the Southern Coast of England* and *Provincial Antiquities of Scotland*, for which Walter Scott was supplying the text.

Financially and professionally secure, Turner in 1817 took his first trip to the Continent since the Peace of Amiens in 1802. He spent most of his time sketching the Rhine, but he also made the increasingly popular pilgrimage to Waterloo. His painting of the battlefield appeared at the Academy in 1818, along with a work based on something he had seen en route through Holland. It was a picture of ships becalmed in a canal in bright daylight, a majestic study in quietude. *Dort* or *Dortrecht* was probably the painting Constable later described as "the most complete work of genius" he had ever seen. Other viewers were almost as impressed, and for a particular reason—the color. The entire canvas seemed a blaze of yellow, compelling attention wholly apart from the subject. "It almost puts your eyes out," one Academician remarked. In *Dort* Turner achieved another major breakthrough toward lasting greatness in art. As in *Hannibal* he had emancipated form, in *Dort* he emancipated color.

The Prince Regent attended the Academy opening of 1818 as usual, but his mind was less on art than on family matters. His daughter Char-

Observation and imagination were interwoven in Turner's art. On a sketching tour through Somersetshire in 1811 he produced the hasty blunt-pencil scrawl at top. Eight years later Turner resurrected it from his notebooks to serve as the starting point for the engraving below, made by a craftsman under his supervision. Three vertical strokes inside a horseshoe shape recalled the masts of fishing boats bobbing by the breakwater. Turner's imagination supplied the cloud banks above and the figures in the foreground. The finished engraving was published in 1820 in a popular series of prints called *The Southern Coast*.

lotte, after a taste of married bliss with Prince Leopold of Saxe-Coburg, had died at 21 the previous autumn in bearing a stillborn son. Although the king was managing somehow to cling to life, the Regent expected any day to ascend the throne. With Charlotte gone, there was no one of his issue to succeed him. He was urged to divorce her madcap mother, Caroline, marry another princess and beget some children. The first idea appealed mightily; his Continental agents were sending back scandalous reports of Caroline's conduct. But he did not especially wish to remarry and sire a new family. He was 56, and had grown so fat that he had to be hoisted up a ramp onto his horse.

Plainly, the responsibility of prolonging the House of Hanover lay with the Regent's brothers—"the damnedest millstones round the neck of any government that can be imagined," Wellington called them. The marriage of the first brother, the Duke of York, had proved barren. The next brother, the Duke of Clarence, had 10 children—by a durable mistress. The next brother, the Duke of Kent, had a durable mistress and no children. Clarence and Kent, both past 50, amiably forsook their partners for proper German princesses. They were both married in the summer of 1818. Clarence's efforts to ensure a dynasty failed, but Kent's succeeded. In May 1819, his Duchess bore a daughter, whom they christened Alexandrina Victoria.

The start of the Victorian era, with its profound changes for England, was less than two decades away. Constable would die on its eve. Turner would survive well into it, as a kind of living legend. But he was not brooding about old age in 1819; the present fully absorbed him. He had decided to take a long look at Italy. Sir Thomas Lawrence, commissioned by the Regent to paint the portraits of Europe's leaders, had written Farington urging that Turner come to Rome: "His genius would here be supplied with materials, and entirely congenial with it." Turner wanted to see not only Rome but Como and Rimini and Verona and, above all, Venice. In August he sailed on a six-month journey that was to open a great new phase of his art.

Constable was taking a fresh tack at home. In the past he had shown only small landscapes at the Academy. This year he submitted a six-foot canvas, a painting now known as *The White Horse*. His motive was practical: he suspected that people regarded a larger work as more of a work of art. In any event, *The White Horse* seemed to awaken viewers to Constable's existence. A scene on the River Stour, showing a bargehorse waiting to be ferried across, it was less boldly executed than some of Constable's smaller landscapes; he was not yet at ease with the larger format. But the simplicity and truth he believed in were there, and people responded. For the first time a critique appeared in which he and Turner were compared as landscapists. Constable, the writer noted, "does not give a sentiment, a soul to the exterior of nature, as Mr. Turner does . . . but he has more of her portraiture."

In November 1819, Constable was at last elected an Associate of the Academy, the rank Turner had reached 20 years before. The time was coming when, to his own great surprise, he would enjoy a triumph Turner never savored: acclaim in another country.

Petworth House from the Park

Sojourn at Petworth

Photographs by Evelyn Hofer

A vast manor house crowded with chattering aristocrats would hardly seem a congenial setting for the gruff, reserved Turner, a man of modest origins whose relationships with others were often difficult. Yet after the death of his father in 1829, he found a welcome home in just such a place, Petworth, an elegant rural retreat whose air of ease and informality lessened his loneliness and enabled his art to flourish.

Petworth was the ornate ancestral estate of one of England's most distinguished families; its grandeur survives to this day, as the photographs on these pages show. Located in Sussex, some 50 miles south of London, Petworth was built on land first ceded to William de Percy, who had crossed from Normandy with William the Conqueror to defeat the Saxons at Hastings in 1066. During Turner's time it was the home of the third Lord Egremont, an eccentric, benevolent peer who was a generous patron of the arts. Turner first visited the estate briefly in 1809 to discuss a commission for a painting, and was a guest again in 1828. But from 1831 until Egremont's death in 1837 Turner often stayed for months at a time and became, in effect, an artist-in-residence.

Egremont enjoyed his role as friend and patron to creative people of Turner's stature; he also entertained Constable and counted among his guests England's leading sculptors and men of letters. The halls of Petworth were decorated with great art of the past and present, including an abundance of classical statuary and an impressive collection of paintings by Van Dyck and Sir Joshua Reynolds.

In this rich historical and artistic atmosphere, Turner's art moved boldly forward. The landscapes he painted there were among his finest, and his interiors caught with perception and wit the country life of England's peerage. More importantly, at Petworth Turner became absorbed with light and color not merely for effect, but as the very subject of his work.

The North Gallery at Petworth

Hallway at Petworth

Rather than flourishing as it did, the vitality of Turner's art might well have been dissipated in the heady country life of England's aristocracy. Like scores of great rural estates, Petworth was constantly besieged by throngs of guests who came to visit for weeks at a time, arriving with carriage loads of luggage and dozens of servants. During the days, the men diverted themselves by hunting or playing billiards, while the women gossiped or took long coach rides to inspect other manor houses. In the evenings, boredom was at least partially avoided by musicales, readings or dances.

While the idle hours may have taxed the imaginations of his fellow guests, they proved a blessing for Turner, giving him the time to observe manor life closely, to study Egremont's art collection and to hike over the rolling grounds in search of dramatic subjects for his landscapes. Among the best of these is the one on the following pages, in which some of the visiting lords are seen playing cricket, oblivious to nearby herds of deer, while two bucks clash in ritual fighting.

In his paintings of interior subjects, Turner also showed a keen awareness of Petworth society. Both his oils and his watercolor sketches *(pages 96-97, 101-102)*, reveal in a charming, humorous manner the lords and ladies at their leisure. These works, which reflect his growing concern with light and color, reached a crescendo in *Interior at Petworth (pages 98-99)*. In this moody study, in which wild beasts and birds roam the once sumptuous halls, Turner was perhaps lamenting the death of Lord Egremont in 1837. Here, light and color dominate, blurring yet illuminating the scene in a style Turner would adopt for some of his greatest works.

Music Party, Petworth, c. 1835

The Lake, Petworth: Sunset, Fighting Bucks, c. 1829-1830

The North Gallery

Painter at an Easel

A Drawing Room

Turner in His Studio

Interior at Petworth, c. 1837

Two Women and a Letter, c. 1835

A Drawing Room

A Bedroom

A Bed: Drapery Study

Flowers in the Library

Life at Petworth was marked by a lack of ceremony that occasionally bordered on chaos. In contrast to most 19th Century English manor houses, Petworth had few schedules and fewer rules. One guest wrote, "Lord Egremont hates ceremony, and can't bear to be personally meddled with; he likes people to come and go as it suits them, and say nothing about it, never to take leave of him." At the same time Egremont was noted for his open-handed generosity—his lavish feasts, including one given annually for the poor, gave rise to legends about his enormous wealth. As a result of his easy-going benevolence, the servants at his estate were held in universal ridicule for being spoiled, old, slow and generally inefficient. Egremont was equally informal in his personal life: he was said to have had scores of mistresses, by whom he had sired many children. The exact numbers are not known, but Egremont finally did take one woman as his wife, after she had borne him six children. The gossip about Egremont, however, only added to the warmth his friends felt for him. As one guest, the painter B. R. Haydon, put it, "The very animals at Petworth seemed happier than in any other spot on earth."

Turner caught this air of happy informality perfectly in his work. His deftly realized scenes—two women fomenting a minor intrigue, one holding a letter behind her back *(page 100)*, guests chatting idly in a drawing room *(page 101)*, studies memorializing rumpled beds *(page 101 and opposite)*—all captured the unrestricted spirits of those who came to visit the elegant mansion.

Stairway leading to Turner's studio

Turner's Studio

In the midst of Petworth's gaiety and confusion, Turner could retreat to splendid isolation without being missed. He was provided with a private studio tucked away on an upper story of the manor house and accessible only by a long flight of stairs *(left)*. In the seclusion of this room, which was well lighted by a tall, arched window *(above)*, Turner was free to work. The serenity of his refuge must have been a great consolation to Turner, who in the recent past had lost not only his father but two other close companions, Walter Fawkes in 1827 and Sir Thomas Lawrence in 1830. In addition to his comfortable quarters, Petworth offered on its ample grounds the delights not only of hunting but also of fishing, a sport of which Turner was very fond.

Egremont must have been as contented with the arrangement as Turner. He was deeply interested in art, and as he grew older he found increasing satisfaction in the works of contemporary Englishmen. This affection reached its peak several years before he died, when he decided he would purchase fewer paintings and sculptures of the old masters and buy more of his countrymen's art. He undertook his new project with his customary grace and generosity, buying and commissioning works by England's greatest painters, from Reynolds and Gainsborough to Blake and Turner. Many of these paintings were placed in different halls around the mansion, but to display his sizable collection to best advantage, Egremont built a special gallery at Petworth *(pages 90-91)*, which at his death held 170 pictures and many fine pieces of sculpture.

Gateway to Petworth Park

V

Travel and Triumph Abroad

Turner crossed the Alps into Italy in September of 1819. The route he took, through the pass of Mont Cenis, was well traveled. With the return of peace the country of the Caesars was again exerting its peculiar pull on the English. "They sweep over the land in swarms, they lodge at every inn, they crowd everywhere to see everything," reported the visiting German poet Heinrich Heine.

Besides ordinary tourists, some of England's most talked-of personalities were in residence. Sir Humphry Davy was in Naples on a mission

Looking up the Grand Canal, Venice, from near the Accademia di Belle Arti, 1819

for the Regent to apply his chemical magic to preserving the scrolls found at Herculaneum. Byron, having sampled the sights and women in other parts of Italy, was living in Ravenna where, he wrote home, "they make love a good deal and assassinate a little." Sir Thomas Lawrence was in Rome painting portraits of Pope Pius VII and Cardinal Consalvi, the city governor, for the Regent's planned gallery of famous men.

Turner's road did not lead at once to Rome. Methodical as usual, he first worked his way across the north of Italy, from Turin to Milan, to Verona and thence to Venice, where he stayed several weeks. Only then did he turn south, through Bologna and Rimini, to Rome. For two months he used the city as a base for exploring Naples, Pompeii, Herculaneum, Sorrento and Salerno. Finally, at Christmastime, he started north again, going to Florence on the first stage of his journey home.

Out of this crowded itinerary came a prodigious number of sketches, nearly 1,500 around Rome alone. Relatively few were watercolors; most were rough pencilings intended to jog Turner's memory on topographical details. Collectively, they reflect a compulsion to record all that the artist's eyes could take in—hill towns and city streets, piazzas and churches and moldering ruins, the excitement of the newly active Vesuvius at Pompeii and the Renaissance repose of the Villa d'Este at Tivoli. Al-

109

though Turner was to return again and again to Italy, he worked on this first trip as if it might be his last.

Breathtaking vistas were only one of his preoccupations; Italy's art treasures fascinated him as well. The long war with Napoleon had deprived him of the chance to see them in the freshness of his student days; now, at the age of 44, he made up for lost time. He haunted the Vatican Museum, sketching its statues and bas-reliefs. He sketched and took notes about drawings by Dürer and paintings by Titian, Correggio and Claude. With a fellow Academician, the well-known sculptor Francis Chantrey, he visited Carrara, whose quarries had served Michelangelo; he later jocularly recalled that the same marble crags that had earned thousands of pounds for Chantrey had afforded him nothing but "a sour bottle of wine and a sketch."

Preceding Turner home to London, Chantrey reported on his industriousness and retailed a bit of gossip to boot. Constable, oddly, was the recipient of this item: it seemed that nobody knew where Turner lodged during his travels around Italy. Why he made a mystery of it can only be surmised. Probably there were sides to Italian life he preferred to explore unobserved. Temptations were rife. Venice alone, which Turner was to wrap in dreams as no artist had ever done, was a sensualist's paradise. The once-proud republic had recently fallen to Austria as a prize of war. In its time of decay its women seemed more alluring, its palaces more golden, its colors more exhilarating than ever before. Byron, relishing its masked balls and moonlit gondola rides, found it an enchanting "Sea Sodom." The passion of Turner's feeling for Venice would be expressed not in words, but in paint *(pages 156-157, 181)*.

Sir Francis Chantrey, with whom Turner visited the Carrara quarries, was renowned for the grace and tender sentiment of his sculpture. In the 1830s his skill brought him both knighthood and a commission from the new king, William IV. Before making a proper marriage, William had lived for some 20 years with an actress, Mrs. Jordan, and had fathered 10 children by her. Upon his accession to the throne, he commissioned Chantrey to make this charming marble statue of the actress and two of their children.

COLLECTION EARL OF MUNSTER

He was back in London in February of 1820—six months to the day he left—and eager to get at his easel. By the time the Academy exhibition opened in May, his *Rome, from the Vatican* was ready for display. One of his largest canvases—about 6 by 11 feet—it shows Raphael on a Vatican loggia, at work on a painting as his mistress stands fondly by; beyond them lies the city. What Turner had intended was an act of homage to the Italian master. What emerged was a busy and diffuse effect lacking in his usual power. He had attempted too much: sentimentality, topography and finicking architectural detail all in one. The work proved a critical fiasco; one reviewer called it an "absurdity" unworthy of Turner's genius. The ridicule must have jarred him; like a shrewd general, he retired to regroup his forces. In the next five years the public was to see only a handful of pictures based on his observations of Italy. The best fruits of his experience there would be slow-ripening.

In any case, he had other things to catch up on after his long absence. His Harley Street gallery—his "Aladdin's palace," he called it—was in disrepair. He leased two adjoining houses and constructed a larger gallery fronting on Queen Anne Street West, around the corner from his old place; this was to be his London address for the rest of his life. Added to his sessions with the mason and the carpenter were meetings of the Academy's governing council, of which he was a member, and a number of Academy social functions too interesting to miss.

One of these was the annual King's Birthday dinner, on the night of

July 3rd. As it happened, Turner and Constable were again seated together. Constable had come quite a distance since their first such encounter seven years earlier. With his recent election as Academy Associate, he was no longer a nonentity in art circles. He was happily married, with a small son and daughter. Suffolk was seeing less of him; both his mother and father had died, and the family home at East Bergholt had been sold. Maria's Grandfather Rhudde, too, had died, without disowning her as threatened. Their inheritances were making it easier to cope with the expenses of a growing household.

What the two men talked of at the Academy dinner is unrecorded, but Italy was certainly of mutual interest. Constable sometimes professed a longing to go there, to see "the living scenes that inspired the landscape of Wilson and Claude," but when he declared that he was "doomed" not to do so it was in a rather cheerful tone. "No," he liked to say, "I was born to paint a happier land, my own dear old England."

Other topics, far from art, were in the air on the night of July 3rd. For the first time in the Academy's 52-year history, the customary toasts at the King's Birthday dinner were drunk to a new sovereign— George IV. George III had finally died while Turner was en route from Italy; the Regent was King at last. The succession picture had changed as well. Little Princess Victoria's father, the Duke of Kent, had died of a sudden lung inflammation in the same week as George III. Now only two aging uncles stood before her as successors to the new King. The most intriguing subject of talk, however, concerned not George's infant niece, but his estranged wife. Caroline, after six years of gallivanting around Europe, had come back to plague him again. No sooner had he become King than she returned to claim her place as Queen.

George was unable to ignore Caroline as he had in the past. Still technically his wife, she was clearly justified in demanding her rights. Moreover, many of his subjects were delighted by her return. George had grown increasingly unpopular during his Regency; Caroline's ready familiarity, her garish makeup and clothes charmed London's raffish elements. Wherever she went in the city, mobs cheered themselves hoarse. They demanded that Londoners light up their houses in a show of support for her cause, and went about smashing windows left dark. But the King was taking steps to rid himself of his nemesis. On July 5th the House of Lords had its first reading of a bill prepared by the King's ministers to deprive Caroline of "the Title, Prerogatives, Rights, Privileges and Pretensions of Queen Consort of this Realm"—and to dissolve the 25-year marriage. Less than 48 hours after the Academy dinner the juiciest scandal in English royal annals erupted into the open.

Caroline's trial—for so the deliberations on the bill were viewed—lasted almost three months, and raised a countrywide uproar. All England was split into Kingites and Queenites, and many feared revolution. In London a double row of fences guarded the House of Lords. Constable sent his wife and babies to the safer and more salutary air of outlying Hampstead. Things in London looked ominous, he wrote to his friend Fisher: "the Royal Strumpet . . . is the rallying point (and a very fit one) for all evil-minded persons." Sir Walter Scott quipped that if Caroline had as many followers of high as of low degree, and the funds to equip them, "I should not be surprised to see her fat bottom in a pair of buckskins and at the head of an army."

Even Caroline's supporters conceded that her behavior abroad had been at least bizarre. At a ball in Geneva she had appeared as Venus, naked from the waist up. At a reception in Baden she had worn half a pumpkin on her head—to keep cool, she explained. On a pilgrimage to the Holy Land she had entered Jerusalem riding an ass, and had founded an Order of Saint Caroline. As grounds for divorce, however, the Bill of Pains and Penalties cited a less eccentric kind of misconduct: her "most unbecoming and degrading intimacy" with "a foreigner of low station." The man in question was one Bartolomeo Bergami, handsome and mustachioed, an ex-quartermaster in an Italian regiment of hussars who had risen rapidly in Caroline's entourage from courier to chamberlain.

What was technically the consideration of an act of Parliament became, in effect, a courtroom spectacle. There were the long-faced peers sitting in judgment, the defendant in a black wig with tossing ringlets, the interrogations by government and defense counsel, and the parade of witnesses. Most of the latter were Caroline's Italian servants, imported by the King's counselors to reveal what they had seen and heard as they passed her bedroom door.

The witnesses backed the most damning charge of the government's case: that Caroline and Bergami had shared a tent on the deck of the vessel taking them to the Holy Land. But evidence was bilingually blurred as to such precise matters as what time of day the Princess and her chamberlain were together there, and how they were clad. The answers were suggestive but ambiguous. By clever questioning the Queen's counselors made the Italians appear confused and unreliable. A farcical note was added by a key government witness who answered most questions put to him by the defense with "*non mi ricordo*"—"I do not recall." The phrase immediately became a catchword on London's streets.

Despite the fuzzy testimony of the Crown's witnesses, most of the Lords were persuaded of Caroline's misconduct; but a royal divorce was the gravest of matters, and many peers were wary of voting for the bill. When the final count was taken, the margin of approving votes stood at only nine. Although the way was clear for sending the bill to the House of Commons, the government instead announced its abandonment. The King's Tory ministers well knew that their slim victory in the upper chamber boded ill for success in the lower, where Caroline's cause was more popular than the King's.

Ostensibly, Caroline was vindicated when the bill was dropped. But after the first jubilant outbursts by her zealous admirers, the pendulum of public opinion swung toward the King. On his coronation day in July of 1821, thunderous huzzas greeted his progress to Westminster Abbey; he was at his most resplendent, wearing a crimson velvet train nine yards long and the dashing plumed hat favored by Spanish grandees. The same day marked Caroline's nadir. Uninvited, she arrived and demanded entry at each of the Abbey's doors in turn; at each she

The remodeling of the Royal Residence at Brighton was a typical extravagance of George IV. Begun about 1800, the project was completed in 1822, under the supervision of Turner's friend John Nash. In the Pavilion's halls, guests might be entertained by a Turkish band—or by the King himself playing the piano, surrounded by ornamental dragons, pagodas and lanterns. Exotic decoration extended even into the Great Kitchen (*below*) where the cast-iron ceiling supports were decorated with sheet-copper fronds.

was barred by a doorkeeper recruited from among the King's old prize-fighter friends. As she rode off, raucous voices in the crowd urged her to "go to Como," where she had frolicked with Bergami. Three weeks later she was dead. Doctors diagnosed the cause as a bowel complaint; friends blamed a broken heart.

As one courtier neatly put it, the King was "affected but not afflicted" by the news. He heard it aboard the royal yacht on the way to Ireland, a trip followed by another to Scotland. Not since his great-grandfather had a monarch set foot outside England; his tour of his realms proved a master stroke. The Irish, although still seething at the continued denial of civil rights for Catholics, could not but give their hearts to a sovereign who sported shamrocks in his hat. The Scots laid on a fortnight of pageantry complete with bagpipes and Highland chieftains. At the King's request David Wilkie, the Scottish artist who had made good in London, painted his portrait in the Stuart tartan.

By the autumn of 1822 the King was back in London and ready to settle down to his reign. No longer merely a stand-in for his father, he now had the full freedom, and the means, to pursue his tastes. That year he completed the architectural wonder for which he is best known: his seaside retreat at Brighton—still standing as a museum—a vast pavilion with domes and minarets, a curious blend of Chinese, Indian and Moorish styles. Other building plans included the conversion of a royal residence in London, Buckingham House, into a proper palace.

Nor did George IV forget his commitment to cultural advance. He gave his father's library of more than 65,000 volumes to the British Museum, as a boon for scholars. Of more moment to artists, he persuaded Parliament to vote £60,000 to buy what became the nucleus of the National Gallery—38 paintings from the collection of John Julius Angerstein, a Russian-born businessman who had been a leading London connoisseur. As far back as Reynolds, painters had urged that there be a gallery to house England's art treasures and stir public pride. The Angerstein collection contained mostly European masters, but also included seven Hogarths, a Reynolds and one work by a living Academician: Wilkie's *Village Festival*. It gave other English artists hope that they, too, might win a niche in the new national repository of art.

Curiously, the idea of a National Gallery had one bitter critic—Constable. Such an institution, he feared, would favor "old" art and thus "suffocate and strangle all original feeling at its birth." He foresaw an end to English painting because its criteria would be set not by nature but by "the manufacturers of pictures."

Constable's stand reflected a basic conflict. He longed for acceptance, yet fiercely fended off attempts to sway his course. He would listen to sitters' opinions about portraits—those were just money-makers. His landscapes, however, were inviolable. On rare occasions he was amenable to making a change if it was suggested by someone special; he once lightened a dark cloud in a view of Salisbury Cathedral because the Bishop considered that feature a needless reminder of rain. But as a rule Constable heeded only his own inner urgings.

Whether he so intended it or not, this attitude helped turn him into an artistic revolutionary. The process had begun with his early vow to paint nature truthfully in an age that preferred it painted theatrically. He never conceded that good art required grandness or even versatility; he believed that it could emerge from everyday subjects and from repeated exploitation of the same scenes. He enjoyed a recurrent sense of discovery along the banks of his beloved River Stour, around the grounds of Salisbury Cathedral, at Hampstead Heath and, later, on the beach at Brighton *(pages 136-137)*. With the same intensity of vision that decades later inspired the French Impressionist Claude Monet to paint 27 studies of light effects on a single haystack, Constable made 52 studies of cloud effects in the Hampstead sky *(page 132)*. "No two days are alike, nor even two hours," he wrote, ". . . and the genuine productions of art, like those of nature, are all distinct from each other."

Constable's technique was as radical for his time as his philosophy. It, too, sprang from his pursuit of nature's truth. In real life one did not see a high gloss on nature; it had roughness and textural variety. Constable represented these qualities by working his brush vigorously, with short, brisk strokes that sometimes went every which way; to add to the effect of an uneven surface, he used generous quantities of paint, sometimes piling it into ridges with his palette knife.

Nature's colors, moreover, are seldom somber or uniform in tone. To record their richness, Constable used bright pigments, and varying tones of each, and often he juxtaposed different hues; in one case he might paint a meadow in various tones of green, in another case in green, blue and yellow. The way he applied colors was his most daring innovation, born of the fact that many of his paintings represented summer scenes around noontime, when the sun was high. Constable did not want to show the sun itself but rather the sparkle and shimmer of its light on the scene below. The method he devised was to apply colors in vibrant little dabs—without any effort at blending. In addition, to convey a sense of "dewy freshness," as he put it, he sometimes strewed the canvas with flecks of white. These highlights became something of a hallmark. His colleagues called them "Constable's snow," or, in Turner's twitting phrase, "Constable's whitewash."

For all his boldness in art, however, the notion of Constable as a rebel would have dumfounded those who knew him. Turner was much more suited to the role; Constable was the very model of a decorous Englishman. Besides, the ultimate effect of his canvases was to soothe rather than to enrage. People grumbled at their "unfinished" look, but seldom stopped to analyze them further. It took two visiting Frenchmen to perceive the forward thrust of Constable's work, and to start the chain of events that made him an artistic sensation abroad.

One man was a critic, Charles Nodier, and the other was Théodore Géricault, leader of the rising French Romantic painters. The picture that captivated them was Constable's *The Hay Wain (pages 120-121)*, a nostalgic scene of some of the most familiar terrain of his boyhood: the River Stour, near the mill at Flatford his father had owned. In the painting a horse-drawn hay wagon crosses the stream; nearby is a farmhouse, and in the background a sunlit meadow. *The Hay Wain* is totally without pretension, drama or even excitement. It caused no special stir when shown at the Academy in 1821. Yet it so impressed Nodier and Géricault that they took news of it back to France, Nodier in a travel book, and Géricault in conversations with fellow artists, including the young Romantic who was to surpass him, Eugène Delacroix.

By the summer of 1824 *The Hay Wain* was hanging in a prominent place at the Louvre, as one of the biggest attractions in the biennial Salon des Beaux-Arts. Its giant leap from obscurity in London to celebrity in Paris was less Constable's doing than the triumph of a persistent French art dealer with the unlikely name of John Arrowsmith, who had appeared at Constable's studio in 1822 and offered £70 for the painting. This was not even half what Constable hoped to get, and he decided not to let himself "be knocked down by a Frenchman . . . it is disgracing my diploma to take so small a price." Early in 1824 Arrowsmith reappeared and offered £250 for *The Hay Wain* and another six-foot canvas exhibited in the interim, *View of the Stour near Dedham.* Constable not only accepted—it was the largest sum he had ever received for his work—but threw in a small painting, *Yarmouth Jetty.*

He had good reasons for taking the second offer. By now he had two sons and two daughters, and a larger and costlier London home. Of more concern, Maria had begun to show signs of the lung affliction that had carried off her mother and brother. She needed long periods away from London's soot and the doctors prescribed the sea air of Brighton. The expense of two households was hardly met by the small family income and picture sales. Constable still had only one steady patron, his friend Fisher, now Archdeacon of Salisbury Cathedral. Fisher had wanted to buy *The Hay Wain*, but gladly yielded to Arrowsmith. With insight he wrote Constable: "English boobies, who dare not trust their own eyes, will discover your merits when they find you admired at Paris."

The French response was more than admiration; in younger artists it was tinged with the joy of revelation. Under the long overlordship of Jacques-Louis David, French painting had been a distinctly solemn affair, classical in concept and staid in color. In the livelier studios of Paris there was seditious talk of the need to abandon history for the present, and to paint with simple, vivid directness. Some of the painters had already been intrigued by the fluency and brilliant color sense of a young English expatriate, Richard Parkes Bonington. Watercolors were Bonington's forte; now Constable's *Hay Wain* confirmed that the new ideas were congenial to a larger format and the medium of oil. Beyond its freshness of color and freedom of brushwork, the painting offered proof that a landscape could be more than the sum of its parts. Traditionalists tended to construct a landscape from separate components of trees, bushes, hills; Constable's work was unified, reducing or eliminating detail wherever detail seemed irrelevant to the whole.

The younger painters reacted as if they had suddenly seen light at the end of a tunnel. After viewing *Hay Wain*, Delacroix rushed off to brighten his own Salon entry, *The Massacre at Chios*, with vibrant color touches such as Constable had used. "This Constable has done me a world of good," he recorded in his journal. Painting *à la Constable* soon became a fashion. Frank imitations of his work were rare; he served, rather, as a catalyst. The great energies in French art that he helped release were to show up in the naturalism of the Barbizon painters, and, four decades later, in the revolution of Impressionism.

Such an outcome would have caused Constable to scoff; even the contemporary acclaim surprised him. His ambitions were limited and his ego easily contained. If fame was to be his, he preferred it among his own countrymen; he had the provincial's wariness of foreigners. Incredulously he wrote Fisher: "Think of the lovely valleys mid the peaceful farmhouses of Suffolk forming a scene of exhibition to amuse the gay and frivolous Parisians." He was pleased but not overwhelmed by his award of a gold medal by King Charles X of France, by glowing critiques of his art in Paris papers, and by reports from returning travelers that he was the talk of the town. Arrowsmith urged him to enjoy his renown in person, and invited him and Maria to come to Paris. Constable toyed only briefly with the thought. "I hope not to go to Paris as long as I live," he wrote. "I do not see any end it is going to answer."

He was far more pleased at the prospect of steady work. Orders from Arrowsmith and another French dealer, Claude Schroth, came with flattering frequency; in all, he made more than 20 paintings for them. And, as Fisher had foreseen, his stock with English buyers began to rise. His confidence bloomed accordingly. A letter to Fisher in 1825 reflected his newfound assurance and also contained an unexpected barb. "My reputation at home among my brother artists is gaining ground," he said, "and I daily feel the honor of having found an original style, and independent of him who would be Lord over all—I mean Turner."

Constable picked an odd time for this sally. Far from thinking Turner supreme, some colleagues had begun to feel that he was, as one diarist noted in mid-1825, "going out of fashion." Fresh in their minds was his humiliation over a royal commission Lawrence had secured for him. Among George IV's decorating projects was a series of paintings of famous English sea and land battles, to be hung in the state rooms of St. James's Palace. Turner, assigned the battle of Trafalgar, had endured a running fire of criticism from naval experts about details of the ships. Although he yielded to their demands, the finished work still did not suit, and was banished to the naval hospital at Greenwich.

Indeed, Turner himself appeared to be dropping out of contention. Twice in recent years he had failed to submit entries to the Academy exhibitions. In the paintings he did display, the one new feature that struck viewers—usually with distaste—was his increasingly "intemperate" color. But on the whole he seemed to have lost his power to shock. So far as his colleagues could see, the pattern of his performance was set: pictures that pleased by their conventionality alternated with those that baffled by their strangeness. In his own oblique way Turner confessed to a sense of staleness. To a friend he wrote in late 1826: "I am a kind of slave who puts on his own fetters from habit . . . an Old Batchelor who puts his coat on always one way."

The same force of habit, however, kept him going at his old pace. The demand for his drawings, to be reproduced in books of English views, remained heavy. Foreign locales, too, were attracting book-buyers' interest. To gather material, Turner made one sketching tour of the Low Countries and another of the Meuse and Moselle Rivers.

In the autumn of 1828 he went back to Rome—this time not to sketch, but to paint. For two months he worked furiously, beginning about ten pictures and completing three. These he decided to exhibit, and more than a thousand Romans flocked to see them. Most left bewildered; by one account they "could make nothing" of Turner's art. In a land aflame with color his exuberant use of it put viewers off. His favorite yellows met with scorn. "The English merchants sell us mustard," one Roman remarked, "and the English artist paints it."

At another time Constable might have derived some wry satisfaction from Turner's reception in Rome, so unlike his own success in Paris. But he was in no mood to gloat, or even to paint. In November of 1828, Maria died of tuberculosis. They had been married 12 years. Their seventh child was still an infant; nursing him had further weakened her. Constable told his older brother: "I shall never again feel as I have felt, the face of the world is totally changed to me." He was to wear mourning for the rest of his life.

His sense of bereavement was all the crueler because a snug future had seemed assured. The year before, he had bought a permanent country retreat at Hampstead, with a view he thought "unequalled in Europe." In March Maria's father had died and left her £20,000. The bitterest pill, however, was that she would never enjoy the honor he had most sought. Three months after her death he was finally elected to the rank of Royal Academician. The evening of the balloting Turner and another colleague came to congratulate him. It was hours later when they parted, in Constable's words, "mutually pleased with one another."

At the Academy exhibition that spring, both Constable and Turner displayed paintings very different from their previous efforts. Constable's was *Hadleigh Castle*, a melancholy evocation of a ruin, with muted colors, a manifest requiem for his marriage. Turner's was *Ulysses Deriding Polyphemus (pages 74-75)*. The essential elements of the Homeric story are clearly visible: the Greek wanderers escaping in their ships, and the one-eyed giant whom they have blinded. But the drama is played in terms of color; blue and red, orange and yellow bespeak the blazing emotions of the protagonists. A triumph of an old theme in a new guise, *Ulysses* marked yet another advance in Turner's art.

In September of 1829 Turner's father died. He was 84, and until his last illness had been his son's devoted helper, watching over his meals and money, managing his studio, even preparing his canvases. Turner felt lost without him. The blow was soon compounded by the death of the painter who had been Turner's longtime champion, Lawrence. In a letter to a mutual artist friend living in Rome, Turner described Sir Thomas' impressive burial ceremony at St. Paul's Cathedral. He had been a pallbearer, and now he wondered, "who will do the like for me, or when, God only knows how soon." Although he was 54, his forebodings were decidedly premature. More than two decades of vigorous activity, and a new flowering of his art, lay ahead.

Portraits
of England

Born in 1776, the son of a grain merchant in the rural area northeast of London, John Constable painted what he knew best, the English landscape, and no one has ever painted it better. His favorite Suffolk countryside—gently rolling, lighted by ever-changing skies, laced by the canals that were then the major inland transportation routes—has come to be known simply as "Constable country." He spent his first 23 years among farmlands so carefully husbanded that the green garden of England at its agricultural peak has become legendary. He was late to find success in his profession, and although he feared that portraiture was his only sure means of providing for his family, he finally broke away to paint nature in his own superb manner.

Constable was repelled by the artificial, prettified landscapes then in vogue, and he initiated an entirely new style: large pastoral scenes painted with a naturalism that his London contemporaries found shockingly crude. It was in France, where his *Hay Wain* and *View on the Stour* were shown in 1824, that his dazzling brushwork and sensitivity to the effects of sunlight first won acclaim. His landscapes shine with light, flashing in brilliant accents from the rich foliage he loved. But more than anything Constable portrayed the panorama of the sky with the skill of practiced observation, and with the precision of the new science of meteorology. It was the sky, he felt, that was "the chief organ of sentiment" in any landscape.

In this view of ripe grain fields framed by tall trees in full summer leaf, Constable, at 50, paid homage to the lush, well-kept Suffolk farmlands where he grew up. Like the shepherd boy in the foreground, he probably drank from the brook as he walked along this lane between his home in East Bergholt and Dedham, where one of his father's mills was located. From the neat green hedgerows to Dedham's square steeple rising above the distant water meadows, the scene spells rural England.

John Constable: *The Cornfield*, 1826

This tranquil portrait of a farm wagon fording the River Stour is the best known of Constable's six major paintings of his native valley. By using a canvas six feet wide, Constable demonstrated his belief that true-to-life landscapes could be every bit as interesting and imposing as the more contrived historical paintings that usually commanded such grand scale. These large pictures were those by which Constable hoped to be judged. Painted between 1814 and 1825, all six concern the few square miles of countryside around his birthplace. And, in a day when some dramatic incident was considered essential to any large-scale picture, Constable included only those local activities that were an integral part of the landscape. Man's presence in Constable's scenes—tilling the soil, herding the animals or plying the waters—is as natural as the land itself.

John Constable: *The Hay Wain*, 1821

121

John Constable: *Dedham Lock and Mill*, 1820

Like every Englishman, Constable was preoccupied with the weather; but unlike most other painters, he made the depiction of atmospheric conditions a major element in his work. In the summer scene on the previous pages, known today as *The Hay Wain*, the qualities of light and color at a particular time of day are so specific that the picture was originally called *Landscape: Noon*. Indeed, each of his six large paintings of the River Stour is characterized as precisely. In *Dedham Lock and Mill* (*above*) Constable softened the red-painted building his father owned with the long shadows of afternoon; raking light floods the canal boats'

John Constable: *Boat-Building near Flatford Mill*, 1815

russet sails and sparkles from the dark foliage of high summer, while the lock's peaceful surface reflects the soft blue of the thinly clouded sky. *Boat-Building near Flatford Mill (above)* shows a riverbank site on property owned by the artist's father where barges were constructed and repaired. Here the leaves are beginning to turn, and a distant meadow is yellowed by the early fall. Constable wrote of such landscapes that he meant "to give one brief moment caught from fleeting time a lasting and sober existence." He succeeded so well in this artistic aspiration that we can almost feel the warm autumn sun on the workman's shoulders.

In this painting, commissioned
as an official portrait of Salisbury
Cathedral, Constable managed to
represent precise architectural
details while still capturing an
atmospheric moment, as he
always tried to in his work. The
picture was ordered by John
Fisher, Bishop of Salisbury and
an old friend of the Constable
family, who stands under the
trees at left with his wife. In 1811
Constable visited the Fishers for
the first time and found not only
new inspiration in the high,
rolling plateau of Salisbury Plain,
but a new friend, the bishop's
recently ordained nephew and
namesake, who was to become
the artist's lifelong confidant.
Constable returned often to the
area, a fruitful source of wide-
skied landscapes, and he painted
the cathedral many times from
various vantage points. He once
said of this painting: "It was the
most difficult subject in landscape
I ever had upon my easel. I have
not flinched at the work, of the
windows, buttresses, etc., etc. . ."

John Constable: *Salisbury Cathedral from the Bishop's Grounds,* 1823

John Constable: *Study of Flowers in a Glass Vase*, c. 1814

John Constable: *Maria Bicknell*, 1816

Constable disliked portraiture in general, and was not particularly good at it, but this charming study of his large-eyed fiancée, Maria Bicknell, done three months before their wedding, shows how well he could succeed when the subject was someone he loved. In desperation at Maria's family's objections to his lack of financial success, he had briefly tried his hand at other portraits, but soon gave it up. He seldom produced still lifes, either, but during this same period he painted several oils of flowers, such as the one at left, which reflects the tender, romantic trend of Constable's intimate thoughts during his frustrating seven-year courtship.

When Constable at last married the girl to whom he was so devoted, the kind young clergyman John Fisher, also newly wed, asked the couple to honeymoon at his vicarage in Osmington, Dorset, on the downs across the bay from Weymouth. Constable, in high spirits, dashed off a group of open-air sketches of the Channel coast, among them this brilliant one of Weymouth Bay under a turbulent sky. Such rapid, on-the-scene studies, done in oil on paper, served the painter as a sort of reference library of scenery, and he often made use of a single sketch, as he did of this one, for several finished works. Artists had long made color sketches as preliminaries for compositions, but Constable was among the first to exploit fully his immediate impressions of nature, making them the real subject of his paintings.

The daring brushwork and free handling of paint that make this sketch so attractive to the modern viewer are also evident in another way in the picture on the following two pages, a cityscape—Constable's only important painting of London and one he took some 13 years to complete. Planned in 1819, when he was working on the large Suffolk river scenes, this vista of the splendid pageantry that accompanied the opening of Waterloo Bridge is a busy urban counterpart to those placid green pastorals. The royal barges and red-coated regiments provided an exceptional color scheme for Constable. This is the picture that was hung at a Royal Academy exhibition next to a misty gray seascape by Turner—and that prompted him to add a bright scarlet buoy to his painting so that it would not appear pallid beside Constable's glittering river scene.

John Constable, *Weymouth Bay*, c. 1816

129

John Constable: *Waterloo Bridge from the Whitehall Stairs, June 18, 1817*, 1832

131

John Constable: *Study of Cirrus Clouds*, c. 1822

Outstanding among Constable's many remarkable oil sketches are the cloud studies he made in late 1822. Like most of the sketches in his private reference portfolio, these swiftly executed oils are almost all annotated with the date, weather conditions, time of day (one is timed at precisely five minutes past five in the afternoon). Constable labeled the lacy formation of cloud represented above, "cirrus," an indication that he was probably familiar with a treatise of 1820 titled *The*

Climate of London, in which the Latin-name cloud classifications in use today were first published. As he saw and recorded constant changes in the sky, so Constable perceived that "neither were there ever two leaves of a tree alike since the creation of the world." His careful pencil, pen and wash studies of specific landscape details, such as the portrait at right of noble elms in a manorial parkland near his birthplace, also reveal his reverence for nature's infinite variety.

132

John Constable: *Elm Trees in Old Hall Park, East Bergholt*, 1817

133

John Constable: *Milford Bridge, with a Distant View of Salisbury*, c. 1836

Though his native valley always remained his favorite scene, Constable sketched and painted wherever he went —at times carefully worked-out compositions, at others quick impressions. The Channel shore, the city of Salisbury, and Salisbury Plain were among the sources of his inspiration. The pencil and pen sketch shown at top is a compositional study done in preparation for a six-foot painting of Brighton Beach; its handsome "parade" lined by waterfront houses and its chain pier frame holiday-makers on the strand and the workaday fishing

John Constable: *The Marine Parade and Chain Pier, Brighton*, c. 1827

John Constable: *Stonehenge*, 1820

fleet that sailed from the mouth of the Steyne. The pencil, pen and watercolor view of Salisbury opposite was later made into an engraving. The pencil drawing of Stonehenge, the mysterious prehistoric monument on Salisbury Plain, was the basis of one of his last pictures, a watercolor exhibited in 1836. The study of Brighton fishing craft on the next two pages shows Constable's concern with precise detail, as well as his spontaneous handling of sky and surf—reflections, once again, of his unquenchable enthusiasm for nature's moods.

John Constable: *Scene on the Beach at Brighton*, c. 1824

VI

A Most Fruitful Decade

Within the brief span of five months in 1830 events combined to give England a new rule, a new spirit and the prospect of a whole new way of life. Suddenly the 18th Century seemed ancient history. The leisured past dimmed before the busy future.

The first event was the death of George IV. His 10-year monarchy had been a case of too little and too late. He spent most of the last half of it in bed at Windsor Castle, drugging himself against the pain of gout and dropsy. His public appearances virtually ceased; having to be laced into his corsets was an agony, and in any case his legs could no longer support him. Yet he still showed flashes of his old flair. As he lay dying, he asked to hear the prayer being said for him in the churches, and pronounced a particular passage "in very good taste." He then planned his own funeral. On June 26 he bled internally, grasped his doctor's hand, murmured "My boy, this is death" and breathed no more.

In London the news provoked neither grief nor joy; there was only the usual bustle in the streets. The city was far handsomer for George IV's efforts, but it would take a later era to be grateful for them. Those who mourned did so less for a man than for a style. A sparkling society required a royal pacesetter, and the new occupant of the throne was clearly anything but.

William IV, the former Duke of Clarence, had become George IV's heir only after the death of their intermediate brother, the Duke of York, in 1827. He was just three years George's junior; at 65 he had little hope for an extended reign. His one ambition, loudly voiced, was to live long enough to see his niece and next in line, 11-year-old Princess Victoria, come of age. This goal was based on his loathing of her mother, the Duchess of Kent, who since her husband's death had assumed great self-importance, and who would become Regent if William died before her daughter reached 18. His hatred sustained the King well; he was to meet his own deadline with three weeks to spare.

His reign had barely begun when his subjects learned what to expect. High living and high fashion were out, economy and domesticity were in. William's first act was to fire his brother's French cooks; plain

English fare was good enough. He thought his coronation a waste of money, and pruned its costs to the point where wits called it the "half-crown-ation." His Queen, Adelaide, the soul of amiability, gamely gave the run of the palace to his bastard children by the actress who had preceded her in his affections. The King presided over this tangled ménage with no apparent unease. He was crude, hearty and blunt, given to sailors' oaths picked up as a young midshipman at sea. In matters of esthetics one of his better-known opinions was that "all pictures of sacred subjects are improper and ought to be destroyed." Measuring him against his predecessor, Englishmen in the arts drew the only possible conclusion: for the duration, royal patronage was a lost cause.

A subtler augury of change appeared in the wake of a new upheaval in France. As July ended, Paris again rumbled with revolution; again a repressive Bourbon ruler, Charles X, was the target, and again civilians confronted soldiers across barricades. But this time there was a crucial difference: frock-coated bourgeois fought alongside workers in rags. Charles X was soon on his way to exile, supplanted by Louis-Philippe, a Bourbon turned democrat, the "citizen-king" whose attitudes were more attuned to those of the rising middle class.

This almost bloodless revolution had repercussions across the Channel. The chief aim of the reform movement that had been simmering in England for decades was political power for the middle class: the vote that would give it a voice in its destiny. The goal now seemed within easier reach; the success of the Parisians, achieved without the noxious terror of the old Revolution, set a hopeful example. In August, in the general election required on the accession of a new king, the anti-reform Tories managed to hold on to their control of Parliament, but with a clear warning—a loss of 50 seats.

September brought another sign of the times: the opening of the Liverpool and Manchester Railway. The occasion was thought to merit the presence of the Tory Prime Minister himself, the Duke of Wellington. The aging hero had as little taste for technology as for democracy; the railway, he felt, would "cause the lower orders to move about needlessly." The lower orders had their doubts too. They argued that God did not mean man to move at the 36-mile-an-hour speed of George Stephenson's locomotive, the *Rocket*—and their fears of retribution were quickly confirmed. As the *Rocket* set off, it struck and killed a former Cabinet minister who had neglected to clear the track.

If there were doubters, there were also those who perceived the railway's potential not just for improving trade and communications, but for advancing the cause of democracy. The reasoning was devious but sound. The bane of political reformers was an archaic electoral system that obstructed meaningful representation in the House of Commons. A Member of Parliament could be elected from a place he neither lived

Early English railways offered three classes of accommodations. Third-class cars were simply open bins, better suited for freight, in which passengers sat on the floor; second-class carriages were dark and uncomfortable with hard wooden seats. First class, however, offered elegant comfort *(below)*. On each car were mounted three cushioned compartments exactly like stagecoaches. And, for those with private carriages, flat cars were provided on which the gentry could ride in accustomed style.

in nor cared about. Some of these areas were known as "pocket boroughs" because of their one-man control. Others, even worse, were "rotten boroughs," once-populated areas that now had almost no inhabitants but still sent one or two politicians to Parliament. Meanwhile, places that had boomed in population had no representation at all.

Rail travel, the reformers hoped, would rouse public indignation at these inequities by providing visible proof: one rotten borough lay right on the Liverpool and Manchester line. Viewing the new roadbed, a businessman who had no one to represent him in Commons hopefully predicted: "A million of persons will pass over it in the course of this year, and see that hitherto unseen village of Newton; and they must be convinced of the absurdity of its sending two members to Parliament, whilst Manchester has none."

Clearly, reform was an idea whose time had come. In November Wellington's Tory ministry fell, and was replaced by England's first Whig government in 20 years, led by the impeccably aristocratic—and pro-reform—Lord Grey. Approval of his appointment lay, as customary, with the King; in a sense, therefore, it was William IV, the least likely of monarchs, who opened the door to the new democracy.

Had the Tories delved deep enough into the King's personality and past, they might better have understood his failure to oppose the new movement. For one thing, William genuinely enjoyed rubbing elbows with his subjects, and often walked London's streets without his retinue. More telling was an experience he had had during his youthful stint in the Royal Navy. William had spent a winter during the American Revolution prowling New York, then still in English hands but ringed by rebel forces. A Yankee plot to capture him, approved by General Washington, had misfired. Perversely, William ever after ranked Washington as the greatest of men next to his first hero, Nelson, and America as a country to admire. Indeed, to be an American, "free and independent," was a wish he voiced even after acquiring his crown.

Deaf to conservative critics, the King gave his support to Prime Minister Grey and to the Reform Bill that was immediately introduced into Parliament. The battle over the bill raged throughout 1831 and well into 1832. Twice the House of Commons approved the measure; twice the House of Lords rejected it, with attendant public fury. Riots, arson and looting scarred the cities, rick-burnings once again scorched the countryside; members of the House of Lords were spat at and assaulted. Finally, in the spring of 1832, Grey hit on a solution. He asked the King to create enough new Whig peers to swamp the opposition in Parliament. The threat alone worked; the Lords did not want their numbers enlarged. On June 4, when the third version of the bill reached the upper house, a hundred Tories led by Wellington abstained, and the bill was swept through.

The measure stripped 87 boroughs of one or both of their Parliamentary representatives and reallocated the seats. Among the beneficiaries were the teeming industrial towns of Manchester, Birmingham, Sheffield and Leeds, none of which had been represented before. Chaotic voting qualifications were also corrected, and some 650,000 people in all were added to the rolls, an increase of about 50 per cent. The voting requirements still kept many of the poor and unpropertied from voting; despite its foes' fears, the Reform Bill was not intended "to give everyone everything." But a vital start had been made.

The spirit of reform roamed everywhere; not even the world of art was sacrosanct. The Royal Academy was belabored in letters to the press for reflecting "the corrupt state and injurious effect of our institutions generally." Specifically, its teaching methods and alleged mercenary outlook were denounced. But the Academy was, on the whole, eminently pleased with itself, and its status quo was maintained.

Still, there were hints of artistic awareness of the times. Both Turner and Constable produced works that were, in their ways, topical. Turner's, shown at the Academy in 1832, was a seascape called *Staffa, Fingal's Cave.* The summer before, on a sketching tour for a new project he had undertaken—the illustration of Sir Walter Scott's collected poems—he had visited Staffa, a tiny storm-tossed island in the Hebrides, and explored the cave where the legendary Gaelic warrior, Fingal, was supposed to have lived. Turner's scene, framed by tall cliffs and crashing waves, reflects many of the aspects of natural force and mystery that he loved; yet what catches the eye is a ship in the middle distance. It is not one of the proud sailing vessels of Turner's previous seascapes, but a small steamer. From one of its funnels a ribbon of black smoke curls toward the cliffs almost defiantly, as if pitting the power of man against the power of nature. To Turner the new technology was not to be scorned; however jarringly it intruded upon land and sea, it had to be accepted as a practical fact.

Constable, on the contrary, longed for what had been. He manifested this feeling in a watercolor of Old Sarum, the most famous of England's rotten boroughs, fated to be eliminated by the Reform Bill. Perched on a hill near Salisbury, Old Sarum had thrived in ancient times as a Roman settlement and then, after the Norman conquest, as a bishop's see; by the 1600s, however, it had become an abandoned ruin and a political anomaly. Explaining his choice of subject, Constable cited a remembered line of verse, "Paint me a desolation." It signaled his own desolate state as well.

Constable was not the sort of man who, like Turner, could make his peace with change. He not only opposed it, he dreaded it. When the Reform Bill crisis was building he took to his bed, so depressed that he seriously alarmed his friend and later biographer, the young American painter Charles Leslie. After one visit Leslie wrote trying to soothe Constable's "useless apprehensions of the future." The attempt at reassurance failed; among other things, Constable feared for the stability of the funds in which he had invested his children's legacy. His reply to Leslie was plunged in gloom. The government, he predicted, was about to fall "into the hands of the rabble and dregs of the people, and the devil's agents on earth—the agitators."

He felt his world crumbling around him; private disappointment added to public calamity. His two French dealers had shut up shop and there were no more orders from Paris. No longer strapped financially,

This oil painting on a lacquered tray is a memento of one of Turner's many joint publishing projects with literary men. In 1831 Turner was asked to illustrate Sir Walter Scott's *Poetical Works.* After an earlier collaboration, Scott had grumped, "Turner's palm is as itchy as his fingers are ingenious." But now, as Turner sketched Abbotsford, Scott's rambling manor on the River Tweed, the two got on so amiably that Scott proposed a picnic luncheon. In memorializing the scene on the tea tray used that afternoon, Turner faithfully captured the sense of the Scottish countryside but did not hesitate to redesign the fanciful castle to his taste, and to bathe it in the warm light of a sun setting in the north.

he did not need the money, but he missed the prestige. He still had no significant standing among his countrymen; for all who admired his work many more dismissed it. A year after becoming an Academician he had suffered a bruising embarrassment. A small oil sketch he submitted for the Academy exhibition, *Water-Meadows near Salisbury*, had been rejected as a "nasty, green thing." The cruelty was inadvertent. Usually Academicians' entries were automatically accepted, but by mischance Constable's painting had come up for the hanging committee's approval unidentified, in a batch of works by outsiders. In token of his election to the Academy's top rank, Constable was on the committee, and so heard the verdict in person. When the truth came out his colleagues moved to reverse the rejection. Constable stiffly insisted that it stand.

Some, no doubt, rejoiced at his discomfiture. He was far from popular. His self-absorption was seen as conceit, and he had a notable talent for tartness. He derided those "high-minded" members of the Academy who preferred "the *shaggy posteriors of a Satyr* to the *moral feeling of landscape*." Individual colleagues also came in for scorching. William Etty, who had beaten Constable in an earlier election for Academician, was known for his sensuous rendition of nudes. Constable, returning from an Academy exhibition, wrote Leslie: "I recollect nothing in the Gallery but some women's bums by Etty R.A." Not above personal sniggers, he was quick to relay a mutual friend's remark that Turner was enjoying "more 'lucid intervals' than usual."

But Constable could be harsh on himself as well. At age 56 he confessed he had not even begun to know himself; professionally he felt becalmed. He was particularly depressed by the commercial failure of a publishing project, *English Landscape Scenery*, which he had launched with high hopes—and his own funds—in 1830. Like Turner's *Liber Studiorum*, it was intended as a kind of compendium of Constable's lifework, reproducing a number of his oil sketches and paintings by the engraving technique called mezzotint.

His perennial champion, Archdeacon Fisher, had cautioned against the idea, pointing out that the charm of Constable's art was color, and that this would be lost in the black, white and gray of mezzotint. Constable had gone ahead nonetheless, and *English Landscape Scenery* was issued in five parts of four scenes each. Sales were meager, and midway through the project Constable foresaw, with some accuracy, that he would be able to dispose of the book only "by giving it away."

Another continuing frustration was a painting now called *Waterloo Bridge from the Whitehall Stairs (pages 130-131)*, Constable's one major try at a London scene in some 30 years of living there. He had toiled over this work off and on for almost half that time, since shortly after the opening of the bridge across the Thames in 1817. In the picture the bridge lies in the distance at the head of a stretch of river, under a broad expanse of sky. River and sky, which predominate on the canvas, were subjects that came easily to Constable, yet the painting bedeviled him at every turn. The trouble was psychological. Despite the open-air elements, he regarded the work as a cityscape, hence not his forte. Never, he complained, had he felt so restless about a picture.

"It has not my redeeming voice," he wrote Leslie, adding by way of explanation, "the rural."

Constable finally showed the painting at the Academy in 1832, having privately voiced the belief that it was an "abortion." Viewers found it even more unfinished than his previous works, and for once Constable agreed. He took without flinching the sharpest critical attack ever leveled at him, one that included Turner in the line of fire. *Waterloo Bridge*, wrote the *Morning Chronicle* reviewer, was just a "piece of plaster," a rank attempt to emulate Turner's "vagaries and absurdities." But, the reviewer concluded, "as Turner is not so funny this year as usual, [Constable's picture] is, among so much dullness, a relaxation to the muscles."

More than the critic realized, there was reason to couple Constable and Turner at this particular point in time, although his venom missed the mark in suggesting that Constable had imitated Turner. Both were nearing 60, and what mattered most to each was the exercise of the fullest freedom in his art. Constable had come to this conclusion out of the recklessness of despair, Turner out of supreme self-confidence. Each was ready to shed the last trammels of tradition, to paint more daringly and creatively than ever before.

Waterloo Bridge may have depressed Constable and its earliest viewers, but its very rawness proved its lasting strength. Despite the time it took to paint, it conveys a powerful spontaneity; not until Impressionism, some 30 years later, would painters record a given moment with more immediacy. Constable was no longer interested in the serenity of a scene but in its vitality. In his few remaining years his brush was to be increasingly uninhibited, his concern for detail even more diminished, his search for the essence of a scene intensified.

For Turner the goal lay in a different direction. His new quest centered on nature's most elusive elements: light and atmosphere. They had long fascinated him, but now capturing them on canvas became a major challenge. In trying to translate these phenomena in paint, he did not restrict himself to any one aspect of them—his attack was all-out. Atmospheric conditions of mist or haze intrigued him as much as air of crystal clarity; moonlight as much as sunlight; direct radiance as much as reflected brilliance on water, land or man-made works. His zeal extended his investigations to artificial light as well; some of his new paintings featured the explosive flare of rockets and fireworks. In one of his night scenes of the period, *Keelmen Heaving in Coals by Moonlight*, the red-gold glow of ships' oil torches dramatically competes with the silvery sheen of the moon on water.

Turner's experiments in light and air are most brilliantly preserved in the paintings of Venice that began to come from his brush in 1833. No place could better have suited his aims. The city lay wide open to sea and sky, peculiarly vulnerable to the elements in times of storm, receptive to their embrace in times of calm. Light and air did not simply seep into Venice, they flooded it, and Venice always responded. Sun-drenched or moon-bathed, wrapped in limpidity or in mist, the Queen of the Adriatic gave off an answering radiance, reflected from a lacework of canals and myriad surfaces of marble and gilt. It was this interaction that Turner caught in his art.

How he caught it remains both a marvel and, in part, a mystery. When he first exhibited his oils of Venice he had not seen the city for 14 years. He returned there briefly in 1835 and in 1840, but altogether he spent perhaps no more than six weeks there. Yet he was able to evoke the ambiance of Venice more powerfully than even its famed native sons Canaletto and Guardi. Few of the city's celebrated splendors are absent from Turner's canvases. The Grand Canal, the Campanile, the Doges' Palace, the stately churches, all receive their due. In recording them Turner had to rely on his extraordinary memory and on the sketches and watercolors he had amassed during his initial visit.

The wonderfully luminous effects he achieved owe a great deal to his mastery of the watercolor medium. Reversing the trend of watercolorists toward making their work look like small oils, Turner set out to make his Venetian oils look like great outsized watercolors. To begin with, he gave his canvas an undercoating of white paint, even as watercolorists usually began with white paper, since a white "ground" on the canvas was the most direct means of avoiding a heavy overall effect. Moreover, Turner banished dark colors from his palette and concentrated on a lighter and more delicate range of hues, with pinks and blues and yellows predominating.

This was all very different from the prevailing practice of oil painters. Most of them began with a dark ground, applied lighter colors atop parts of it, and relied on contrasts of light and shade—chiaroscuro—to build up form. But the mere thought of chiaroscuro in Venice must have pained Turner. Sheer radiance was what he sought, and he found it by superimposing light colors on white. In *The Dogana and Santa Maria della Salute (pages 156-157)*, by planting the marble domes of the church against a bank of clouds, he even went so far as to paint white on white—an artistic audacity almost unheard of at the time.

Turner applied his colors, again adapting the watercolorists' technique, by building thin layer upon thin layer, and wielding his brush more gently than in earlier works. To achieve the tremulous effect of his Venetian canvases—as if both light and air were ever so faintly vibrating—he employed both glazes and scumbles. A scumble is a thin, broken layer of opaque pigment, usually containing a good deal of white; when used over a dark color, it has a softening effect. A glaze is a transparent film that does not obscure the color over which it is laid, but combines with it to produce a glowing variation of the original hue. By the inventive and subtle manipulation of these devices Turner created the endless gradations of light that are the glory of his Venetian works.

But what went into the glazes and scumbles, or into the mixtures that produced the pearl-like iridescence of his scenes of Venice shrouded in mist, Turner never disclosed. Some of the ingredients may well have been unorthodox; he was once detected preparing to mix powdered pigment with what seemed to be stale beer. Such a revelation, however, was rare indeed. As a contemporary biographer noted, Turner's studio was "hermetically sealed" against prying eyes.

A number of Turner's Venetian paintings were discovered only after he died. He may have planned further work on them, he may have been unable to sell them, or he may simply have kept them for his own gratified remembrance of the city he loved. In any case the outside world had much else by Turner to admire. The demand for his drawings, for reproduction in books, was still high. When seeking his services as illustrator for Scott's collected poems, the publisher wrote Scott, with unflattering frankness, that with Turner he could guarantee a sale of 8,000 copies, without him fewer than 3,000.

Other publishers were as happy to trade on Turner's name and fame. His collaboration with Scott was followed by similar ventures with two other popular contemporary poets, Samuel Rogers and Thomas Campbell. Of more lasting interest, Turner illustrated an edition of Byron's works, issued a decade after his tragic death in 1824 during the war of Greek independence. Byron's impact on Turner led him further to produce two paintings based on *Childe Harold's Pilgrimage*, the epic account of the poet's wanderings through Europe. Turner may well have read into the romantic sweep of Byron's verse a striking identity of experience, for he, too, had wandered far and wide, reverencing nature's grandeurs and pondering human fragility.

Books of views also occupied him. New folios appeared of his highly successful works of the 1820s, *Picturesque Views of England and Wales* and *Rivers of France*. He also undertook a new opus entitled *Turner's Annual Tour—Wanderings by the Loire and the Seine*, published in three volumes. An entire series of volumes on the scenic beauties of Europe's other great rivers was planned and even advertised. Eventually the project fell through, but it sent Turner off on sketching tours of hitherto untried territory along the Elbe and Danube and around Berlin, Prague and Vienna. Although he had begun to complain of signs of aging, he manifestly enjoyed the exertion. To an English fellow passenger on a coach during one journey he seemed tireless, a "funny, little elderly gentleman . . . continually popping his head out of the window to sketch whatever strikes his fancy."

Amid his labors Turner found time for frequent and protracted stays at Petworth, the baronial home of an increasingly devoted patron, Lord Egremont. Petworth lay about 50 miles south of London, and an infinite distance from Turner's modest beginnings. It was—and is—one of England's great houses, a stately stone pile set in a park measuring 14 miles around, and housing a magnificent treasure of Old Masters, antique statuary, Italian Renaissance and French furniture, Chinese porcelains and Georgian silver.

Petworth, however, was less like a museum than a lively, sprawling inn, with armies of guests and servants constantly coming and going. Its master, George Wyndham, third Earl of Egremont, was very large, very rich and very generous. His motto was "Live and let live." From his eighties he could look back at a lifetime of singleminded dedication to what one admirer described as "the dispensation of happiness." Aiding him in this pursuit was a £100,000-a-year income inherited with his title at the age of 12. As a young rake he had lavished gilded carriages on a famous French courtesan. As master of Petworth he had launched the annual habit of entertaining some 6,000 of his poorer neighbors at a feast where, an eyewitness recalled, "Plum puddings and loaves were piled high like cannon balls."

Less fleeting causes also elicited Egremont's bounty. One was the promotion of scientific principles of farming. Another, still closer to his heart, was the fostering of English art. He had long since added Reynolds and Gainsborough and Wilson to his stunning inheritance of works by Van Dyck and the Dutch, French, German and Venetian schools. In time he began to concentrate solely on living English painters. He liked both their work and their company; open house at Petworth was an integral part of his philosophy of patronage.

Many Academicians availed themselves of the pleasure. Constable did so, but only briefly. He confessed to his confidant, Leslie, that he felt "awkward . . . with the great folks." In theory Turner should have felt at least as uncomfortable. In fact he flourished at Petworth, honored and pampered. His host set aside a handsome room for Turner's exclusive use *(pages 104-105)*, and when he was painting in this retreat it was off limits to all but the Earl himself, who would announce his approach with a prearranged number of knocks.

Despite their disparity of background, the two men were birds of a feather—careless of dress, blunt in speech, masking complexity behind a surface simplicity. They could afford to be completely honest with each other. One day Turner, whose ability as a painter of faces and figures was scarcely up to his skill in other respects, presented Egremont with *Jessica*, a fanciful portrait of Shylock's daughter. Egremont was less than enthusiastic about the picture. "Turner," said the Earl, "I want a picture painted when you have time, but remember, none of your damned nonsense!" Turner took the blast in stride. He did not need to be reassured of Egremont's esteem any more than Egremont needed to be reminded of Turner's genius.

His enduring artistic tribute to the years at Petworth was a series of oils and watercolors *(pages 93-103)* memorializing the beauty outside its doors and, even more notably, the life inside. Absorbed in landscapes, Turner had seldom attempted interiors other than in quick pencil sketches. The triumph he achieved indoors at Petworth was won with the same means that served him so well in his interpretations of nature: color and light. In Turner's scenes of the rooms at Petworth color and light are not intended to define either objects or figures, except by seeming chance. Their purpose, magnificently realized, is to seize the spirit of Petworth, its vigor and vibrancy and joy.

Visits to Petworth invariably renewed him, and it was shortly after a stay there in the autumn of 1834 that he painted two of his best-known masterpieces. In London, on the night of October 16, fire swept the Houses of Parliament, gutting the ancient palace where lords and commoners had for 600 years held their deliberations. Among the watchers crowding the banks of the Thames many drew special pleasures from the spectacle; time had not calmed the tempers stirred by the Reform Bill crisis. The writer Thomas Carlyle, soon to be acclaimed as England's foremost historian, heard a cheerful Cockney voice cry "There go their *hacts!*" as tongues of flame shot up from the House of Lords. "The crowd," Carlyle added, "*whew'd* and whistled when the breeze came as if to encourage it . . . A man *sorry* I did not anywhere see."

Turner was also on hand, busily sketching from across the river, darting from one vantage point to another. Besides numerous pencil sketches he made nine in watercolor, in such haste that the blank pages opposite them in his sketchbook show the resulting blots. Perhaps he remembered a night in 1792 when another disastrous fire had destroyed one of London's great buildings, the Pantheon; Turner, a very junior student at the Academy, had not troubled to take a firsthand look until the next morning, and then produced a sedate drawing that featured firemen in Neoclassical pose. In the prime of his art four decades later he knew better. Fire itself, in all its ferocity, dominates the two oils of the event he exhibited in 1835, one a view from directly across the Thames, the other a view from down river at Waterloo Bridge *(pages 154-155).*

Neither Turner nor any other Londoner of his time had ever seen such a fiery rampage. For Turner, inevitably, it invited comparison with everything else he had observed and loved of nature at its most furious and elemental, in high seas and mountain storms and Alpine avalanches. Fire, moreover, could be painted in terms of the color and light that now obsessed him beyond any other aspect of his art. It offered a new field to conquer, a theme he would return to again and again.

Constable also witnessed the burning of Parliament, but his response was different. He arrived at the scene by hackney coach with his two oldest boys, John and Charles, then 17 and 13, and watched it wholly as a spectator. That he had thought to take his sons along with him indicates the importance he attached to the event as a memorable bit of history. But he did not view it as a challenge to his artistry. In time he did turn out some watercolors of the House of Commons as it looked both during and after the fire, but that was the extent of his involvement. Possibly the critical fiasco of *Waterloo Bridge* made him wary of another attempt at a London scene, or perhaps the theme of violence unleashed —so irresistible to Turner—was not one that Constable cared to perpetuate in the name of art.

In any event Constable had a new interest: the lecture platform. Long persuaded that landscape painting was too little valued, he had determined to try to elevate it in the public mind. He had begun his campaign in 1833 with a lecture before the Literary and Scientific Institution of Hampstead, reviewing the history of landscape painting and its illustrious practitioners. In 1835 and 1836 he returned to the campaign with several more lectures, including four in London in a setting not usually associated with art, the Royal Institution, founded in 1799 for the "promotion, diffusion and extension of scientific knowledge."

For his appearance there Constable could thank his son John, a student at the Institution laboratory under the eminent Michael Faraday, discoverer of some of the basic laws of electricity and magnetism. Faraday arranged the lectures on hearing that Constable believed that painting was as much a science as an art. This viewpoint was probably

When fire reduced to rubble the Old Palace of Westminster, Parliament's meeting place, on the evening of October 16, 1834, Turner was among the thousands of Londoners who had thronged to the spectacle. Turner's interest was professional, leading to such paintings as the one reproduced on page 154; the mob came to savor what seemed proper retribution for Parliament's unpopular policies, and became so excited that the army had to help restore order.

RECORDS ROOM, HOUSE OF LORDS, LONDON

an inescapable outcome of his early vow to seek truth. He began his first lecture with the assertion that "imagination alone never did, and never can, produce works that are to stand by a comparison with *realities*." He ended his last lecture with the declaration that "painting . . . should be pursued as an inquiry into the laws of nature." He was pleased with his reception and planned to expound on his ideas at another lecture in the summer of 1837.

He did not live to deliver it. On March 30th of that year he attended the first general meeting held by the Royal Academy in the National Gallery's imposing new home in Trafalgar Square. The Academy's annual exhibition impended, and the next day Constable worked on his entry, *Arundel Mill and Castle*, a scene of a region he had only recently come to know and admire, Sussex. Late that night he woke in acute pain and died within half an hour. During the past decade he had suffered from sieges of rheumatic fever, but a post-mortem failed to disclose the actual cause of his death. He was buried in a vault in the Hampstead churchyard, beside his beloved Maria.

Under the watchful eye of his friend Leslie, Constable's sketches were saved from public auction, at which they might have gone for a few shillings per bundle, and secured for his children. It was Leslie, too, who sparked a subscription campaign to buy one of Constable's large unsold paintings to present to the National Gallery. The work chosen was *The Cornfield (page 119)*, painted in 1826, an affectionate recreation of a Suffolk lane Constable had tramped as a boy. His friends subscribed 300 guineas for it—more than he had commanded for any painting in his lifetime. The National Gallery, which Constable had seen as a deathtrap for original talent, accepted *The Cornfield* with "great gratitude" in December of 1837.

By then England was relishing the excitement of a new reign. William IV had died in June; Victoria was Queen. At 18 she was less than five feet tall, blue-eyed and fair-haired but not especially pretty. Her subjects thought she was taking hold remarkably well; the first order she had given as Queen was to move her bed out of her mother's room, where she had always slept, and in other ways she was showing a mind of her own. Art circles, ever alert to changes in royal tastes, detected a straw in the wind when a knighthood was proffered to the Academician Edwin Landseer, whose portrait of a dog, *Mustard*, had won recent kudos as "an immortal picture."

Among the artists on the Queen's honors list, Turner's name was conspicuously absent; his art was clearly too iconoclastic to suit the royal taste. But one signal distinction did come to him in 1837, by way of the powerful sea piece he had produced in 1802, *Dutch Boats in a Gale*. It was the only work by a living painter to be represented in a British Institution show of Old Masters.

The honor emphasized the position Turner was accorded by his colleagues if not by his Queen. He was now indisputably the Grand Old Man of English art. The role was owed mainly to his towering repute, but also to simple survival; not many of his contemporaries remained.

To younger painters he was both a colossus and a character. Stu-

In 1838, the year after Victoria acceded to the throne, this flattering portrait of her appeared as the frontispiece to an annual *Book of Beauty*. Such handsomely bound collections of engravings of pretty, well-dressed girls were avidly read by fashionable English ladies. Although the little Queen's face and form were hardly inspiring, she was possessed by a sense of duty and radiated a high-mindedness that impressed her subjects and characterized her 63-year reign.

dents at the Academy school viewed him with mingled awe and mischief. Turner finally resigned as Professor of Perspective in 1837, to everyone's relief, including no doubt his own; but he still taught as a so-called Visitor to the school. This assignment, rotated among the Academicians, was intended to give fledglings the varied wisdom of their elders. How much they learned from Turner, aside from his enigmatic hints for correcting specific errors, is debatable. He could not put into teaching the passion he poured into painting, nor is it likely that he wanted to. By one student's account his classmates spent much of their time, when Turner was Visitor, trying to sneak a likeness of him on the margins of the drawings they were supposed to be finishing. He was a choice subject, with his hawk nose and quizzical glint and head too big for his body; age had accentuated his resemblance to Punch. But Turner would intuitively spot a would-be portraitist and promptly shift his posture.

He spared the culprit any rebuke, however. For behind his brusque manner lurked a sense of humor and a sentimental attachment to the Academy and all its practices. It satisfied a hunger for the family life he had never enjoyed. He made a revealing remark on being told of the suicide of Benjamin Haydon, a cantankerous colleague who had labored hard to undermine the Academy. "He stabbed his mother," was Turner's curt response.

His own loyalty was fierce. He cut a familiar, if odd, figure both at Academy business meetings and its festive affairs. These, and an occasional dinner, boating party or picnic with a few colleagues he liked, made up virtually all of his known social life. With Lord Egremont's death in late 1837 Turner no longer went to Petworth. Apparently it never occurred to him to return any hospitality. Those who ventured to drop in at his house on Queen Anne Street did so only to inspect his gallery, and even then found it a trial.

After nearly two decades the house had taken on some of the strangeness of its occupant. Sarah Danby's niece Hannah still kept house for Turner, and age had not improved her skills. Thick dust lay on dilapidated furniture. Turner would shuffle downstairs in slippers, and when he showed visitors around the gallery he could be almost rudely vigilant. One young lady noticed several spots on a painting and offered Turner her cambric handkerchief to rub them out. As she told the story, "the old man edged us away, and stood before his picture like a hen in a fury."

In the late 1830s Turner's friends began to suspect that he also lived someplace else. He would drop out of sight for weeks at a time, then as abruptly reappear. The mystery intrigued them and they made a game of trying to trap him. After an Academy session they would offer to walk him home; he would plead an engagement. They would follow him; he would duck around a dark corner. The secret was cracked by a colleague who happened to call on Turner at his gallery just as he was going out. Unexpectedly cordial, Turner invited the painter and his young son to walk with him. It was a long walk, all the way to Chelsea, on the southwest fringes of London. The goal was a small house on the

Thames, at No. 119 Cheyne Walk—a street that was later to boast another resident prickly genius, James McNeill Whistler. Turner's hideaway was shabby but it had one great asset: a spectacular view both up and down the river. The outlook so pleased him that he had a passageway cut from his top-floor bedroom to the roof, where he could sit and feast on unobstructed stretches of sky and water.

In later years the boy who had accompanied his father and Turner to Chelsea recalled that they had been served bread and cheese and porter by someone he described as an "attendant . . . an old woman." To youthful eyes Sophia Caroline Booth no doubt looked ancient. Actually she was fortyish, more than 20 years younger than Turner, a cheerful, buxom brunette with a high tolerance for Turner's crotchets. Mrs. Booth may have lacked schooling, but a letter to her from Ruskin, long after Turner's death, could hardly have been written to a dolt. Ruskin urged her, in a tone that indicated he was addressing a person of substance, to "cast aside with contempt and carelessness" Thornbury's scurrilous biography.

Apparently Turner had known her well since the early 1830s. By then she was once widowed, mother of a son, and married to her second husband, with whom she ran a lodging house in Margate. The little seaside town was a quick run from London and offered Turner an inexpensive haven between stops at Petworth. At that time his personal affairs had been in flux. His father was gone, and his relations with Sarah Danby had evidently worsened beyond repair. In a will he made in 1831 he left her a niggling £10 per year for life, and later revoked even that, along with two more liberal annuities for their daughters. Whether he and Sarah simply drifted apart or quarreled is uncertain. In any event Sophia Booth, with her even temper and good looks, increasingly filled the gap in his life. Her second husband died in 1833, and in time she moved to Chelsea, closer to Turner's home base.

Judging from the few clues, they made a congenial couple. Turner was never one to let his guard down, but he seems to have trusted her fully. He went to some pains to further her son's training as an engraver —raising rumors that he was the youth's real father. In addition, he was unusually generous in giving Sophia a number of his oils and drawings; a decade or so after he died she put most of them on sale at Christie's in London and realized nearly £4,000. She well deserved his favor. Under her care Turner saw the doctor and dentist when needed, and he also looked better—his clothes brushed as never before, his appearance in public sometimes even spruce.

To his Chelsea neighbors Turner was known only as Mr. Booth. A puckish whim spurred him to take Sophia's name, and it was obviously convenient as well. Locally, he was believed to be a retired seadog, because of his ruddy face and rolling gait; some called him "Admiral." At the little house he painted or, when a sunrise or sunset excited him, sketched on the roof. His pace was less urgent; he took time to nap and to thumb through *The Art Journal* and *The Illustrated London News*, and occasionally he and Sophia went for a stroll or a ride on the river. He had a measure of contentment long denied him.

Making Moo into Matter

Turner's later paintings—those by which he is best known today and for which he was ridiculed in his own time—are haunting compositions of indistinct forms that emerge through brilliant veils of light and color. They are not simply shimmering exercises in paint, but subjective studies of nature, embodying the insights and techniques that Turner spent a lifetime acquiring. Imaginative and daring, these paintings thrust Turner to the forefront of 19th Century art. Many of his contemporaries found them baffling, and even to the modern viewer they may remain elusive in meaning and tantalizing in mood. But they are fascinating to the eye and mind.

Ostensibly, these later works were based on conventional themes that had served Turner well in the past. Mostly they are traditional scenes from antiquity *(right)* or views of cities, castles or country estates. In style and mood, however, they go far beyond convention; infusing them are Turner's visions of a world sometimes buffeted by howling gales, sometimes ablaze with dazzling sunlight, sometimes enveloped in billowing mists. As a result, they often present not a clearly defined subject but an ambiance, an aura. His real themes were the elements —light, air, wind, water and fire—at their most violent and their most sublime. But his treatment of them was too startling for most 19th Century English art buyers. As a result Turner, the most formidable artist of his day, left many of his final works unappreciated and unsold.

Quite late in his career, Turner was still painting works that mixed a naturalistic landscape with an event from classical history. In this scene of ancient Greece, Phryne, a beautiful courtesan, is carried to the baths in a gilded chariot *(lower right)* amid a jubilant procession. Two leaders of state, Demosthenes and Aeschines, debate politics at left. Turner's interest, however, is much less in the action than in the sunlight in the foreground and the mist-shrouded cityscape in the distance.

Phryne Going to the Public Bath as Venus: Demosthenes Taunted by Aeschines, 1838

153

Burning of the Houses of Lords and Commons, 16th October, 1834, 1835

When the houses of Parliament were consumed by flames in 1834, the 59-year-old Turner found a subject that seemed to have been made for him. All his life he had been fascinated by the fury of nature's forces; he also saw man's struggle against these elements as futile. Now one of his country's own great monuments was being destroyed by fire—a scene rich with drama and symbolic overtones. As he watched the old palace that housed Parliament burn, he transcribed the event directly in a series of watercolors, brushing so hurriedly that he blotted some of his paintings together on the pad. Later, working from these quick sketches, he completed and exhibited two oils, including the one at left—in which fire, sky and water blend to form an apocalyptic scene. The tension here between a depiction of an actual event and the subjective lure of sheer light and color charges the atmosphere. Although the event is the burning of Parliament, it is the tower of flames shooting into the night sky and reflecting in the quiet Thames that is the real center of attraction.

155

The Dogana and Santa Maria della Salute, Venice, 1843

Another subject that seemed ready-made for Turner was the fairy-tale city of Venice. The artist had visited Italy in 1819, a trip that resulted in a vast number of watercolors and drawings that captured the bright realities of the sunny land as candidly as snapshots. Returning several times between 1829 and 1840, Turner also produced many paintings, but the mood of these was completely different from the earlier Italian sketches. Then he had been concerned with the look of the land; now he was more interested in its character. And of all the Italian cities that he visited, it was Venice that captivated Turner most.

Situated in an Adriatic lagoon like a giant lily pad on a pond, Venice was a blend of land, water and stone; laced by myriad canals and visited alternately by soft mists and brilliant sunlight, the city communicated a presence that was altogether magical. Even Venice's political past added to its romantic luster. Once a mighty seaport with an empire of its own, the city in Turner's day was but a forgotten corner in the Austrian realm and a playground for tourists—a fabled city living on fading beauties and lost hopes. Looking across the Grand Canal toward one of the city's many lovely churches to paint the view at left, Turner saw both the reality and the dream.

157

One day when Turner was riding a
train during a violent rainstorm, he
thrust his head out a window and sat
for fully 10 minutes watching the
engine race through the downpour. In
transcribing his impressions to canvas
later, he created one of his most
powerful and best-known paintings:
*Rain, Steam, and Speed: The Great
Western Railway (right)*. To convey the
sense of speed, Turner showed the train
tracks receding sharply into the
distance and racing off the corner of the
canvas in the right foreground; the
train itself is a streak of movement,
with only the black smokestack defined
as a focal point. The major force in the
painting, however, is the rain that
sweeps across the entire canvas,
blurring machine, tracks and trestle
into a landscape of motion and mood.

158

Rain, Steam, and Speed: The Great Western Railway, 1844

159

Turner's great technical facility enabled him to suggest as much in his paintings as he actually showed. Long a master of watercolors, he was also gifted at transmitting in oils the evanescence of colors, which seem almost to float over his white canvas backgrounds. This effect was brilliantly realized in *Norham Castle (right)*, a work that has the diaphanous quality of a watercolor sketch, yet the grandeur of an oil painting.

The study seems devoid of solid objects: the castle is an amorphous blotch of blue in the background; the cow grazing in the foreground provides a sense of scale but is as indistinct as a reflection in a pool. With a few exceptions, Turner's brush has caressed the canvas like a vapor: the entire landscape is blurred, containing dimly perceived forms that emerge through the haze of glowing color. The hues are pale and cool, in direct contrast to the brilliant colors favored by Turner only a few years before *(pages 93-102)*. Yet Turner's new-found palette captures eloquently the tranquillity of a country sunrise.

160

Norham Castle, Sunrise, c. 1835-1840

161

Shade and Darkness: the Evening of the Deluge, 1843

Turner constantly sought new ways to bring his personal visions to life through color. In two of his late paintings, shown here, he used elements from the Bible as his subjects and interpreted them, using a recently translated theory of color devised by the German poet Goethe. In *Shade and Darkness (above)*, pairs of animals file through the rain toward Noah's ark, a vague shadow at the center of the painting. The colors are those Goethe called "minus" colors—blues, blue-greens and purples— which in his theory represented "restless, susceptible, anxious impressions." In Turner's circular composition, in which a flight of birds describes an arc over the scene,

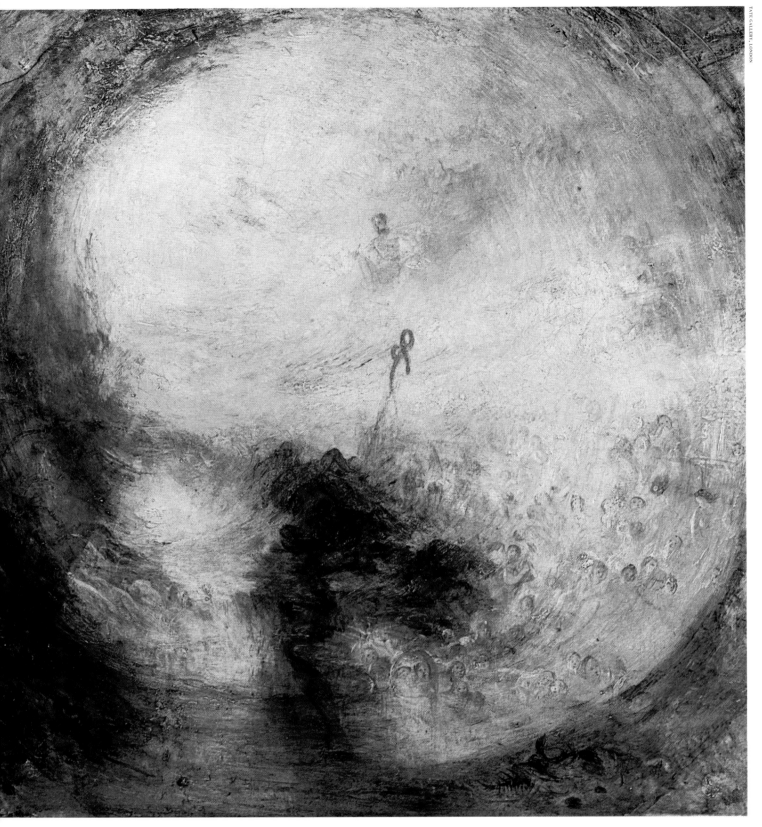

Light and Color: the Morning after the Deluge, 1843

these colors form a tunnel toward the light at the center, drawing the viewer into the vortex.

In a companion piece, *Light and Color (above)*, Turner painted with Goethe's "plus" colors—the reds, yellows and greens the poet associated with warmth, happiness and gaiety. In this picture, the sun has burst forth after the rains; the earth is a green outcropping from which a serpent uncoils; amid the swirling light, a beardless Moses writing the Book of Genesis on a tablet materializes at the upper center. In contrast to *Shade and Darkness*, the warm colors seem to fly outward, carrying the center of the painting toward the viewer.

VII

Turner's Bequest

Late on a summer day in 1838, standing at the rail of a fast new steamer that plied the Thames between London and Margate, Turner beheld a sight that was to inspire his best-loved work. Moving majestically upstream was the old warship *Temeraire*. Every Englishman knew her history: she had fought under Nelson at the Battle of the Nile in 1798; seven years later, with all the daring her name implied, she had notably served England's cause at Trafalgar. To the *Temeraire*, second in the fleet's line of battle, had gone the glory of avenging Nelson's death, blasting the enemy vessel that had raked his flagship *Victory*.

Now, after 33 more years, the *Temeraire* was on a final mission of destruction—her own. Stripped of her sails and 98 guns, her hull rotting beneath a last perfunctory coat of paint, she was en route from the naval base at Sheerness to a private wrecker's shipyard, to be broken up for her heart-of-oak timbers and copper fittings. A sturdy steam tug guided her. Above this agent of the new age of speed the *Temeraire* loomed tall and still proud, taking the salute of a brilliant setting sun, going to her doom with a queen's grace.

Turner's *The Fighting "Temeraire" tugged to her last berth to be broken up (detail, opposite)* appeared at the Academy in 1839. The theme would have stirred the English at any time, but at this stage its patriotic appeal was special. The reign of Victoria was just under way, and the pains of transition were multiple. The girl on the throne was enamored of her Prime Minister, the worldly Lord Melbourne, and under his suave tutelage she seemed to be learning more social gossip than statecraft. Wiser heads around her were worried; the problems beyond the palace were pressing.

Bigness lay at the root of most of them. The growth of England's realms abroad had complicated the colonial picture; before Parliament was a startling report by Lord Durham, just returned from Canada, urging that all the colonies be made self-governing. At home, the growth of England's economy had spread the seamier aspects of industrialism. In a recent novel, *Oliver Twist*, a young writer named Charles Dickens had offered a chilling look inside the compulsory workhouses for the

Turner captured a poignant bit of British history when he painted the grand, ghostly hulk of the *Temeraire*, a ship of Nelson's glorious fleet, being led on her last voyage to the scrapyard by a tug belching smoke and soot.

The Fighting "Temeraire" tugged to her last berth to be broken up, 1838, detail

idle poor. The Queen herself had read the book and found it "excessively interesting," but apparently thought it pure fiction. Others recognized its sordid truths, and were giving ear to a radical movement called Chartism. Its "People's Charter" demanded the vote for every male citizen, as well as further advances over the political reforms of 1832. Some Chartist leaders openly favored violence to gain their ends.

Wherever they turned, the English saw only complexities. The nation was nearing the pinnacle of world power. To look forward was tantalizing, but to look back was reassuring. Turner's *Temeraire* fulfilled a widespread wish to be reminded of a time when things were simpler, when the thorniest of problems could be solved by valor alone.

Ironically, the painting by any other name might well have been hooted down. Had Turner titled it merely *Ship on the Thames*, viewers might have paid less heed to the subject matter and more to the artistic liberties he had taken. Virtually every color on his palette, hot as well as cold, had been put to use. Added to this assault on the senses was a snub for sticklers for detail. Choosing to portray the *Temeraire* as a ghost ship, Turner had dropped all pretense at precision. The result, one marine painter protested, was nothing more than "a diaphanous spectre of mist and moonbeams, rigged with cobwebs."

Few others complained. Whatever means Turner had used, in this case they splendidly served the end, a paean to heroism. He was never more vindicated in his belief that color was meant not to describe, but to arouse and excite. His loudest plaudits came from a newcomer among London's reviewers, William Makepeace Thackeray. Thackeray's famous satirical novels lay in the future; now he was whetting his ax as critic for *Fraser's Magazine*, under the alias of Michael Angelo Titmarsh, Esq. Usually, Turner's efforts repelled him; he was not above hinting at the painter's lunacy, or likening an effect in one work to "huge, slimy, poached eggs." *Temeraire*, however, struck him differently.

"It is absurd," he wrote, ". . . to grow so politically enthusiastic about a four-foot canvas, representing a ship, a steamer, a river and a sunset. But herein surely lies the power of the great artist. He makes you see and think of a great deal more than the object before you; he knows how to soothe or to intoxicate, to fire or depress, by a few notes, or forms, or colours, of which we cannot trace the effects to the source, but acknowledge the power." Thackeray summed up with equally keen insight into Turner's essential intent with color. "When the art of translating colours into music or poetry shall be discovered," he declared, Turner's *Temeraire* "will be found to be a magnificent national ode or piece of music."

In a way Turner may have seen himself in the painting: a veteran warrior near journey's end. Certainly, except for *Temeraire*'s success, his professional fortunes appeared to be on the wane. Over the years his most lucrative source of income had been the publishing trade. The widely popular reproductions of his drawings were made from engravings on copper, but now this process had a rival in the newer method of engraving on steel. It was cheaper, and permitted many more impressions from a plate. Turner detested their quality; he felt that steel lacked cop-

Mid-century English writers turned increasing attention to the cruel plight of the working classes. Among the earliest novels on the subject was Mrs. Frances Trollope's *The Life and Adventures of Michael Armstrong the Factory Boy*, published in 1840. Attempting to arouse the consciences of her middle-class readers, who believed as strongly in progress as in morality, the author noted that the horrors she described were not fictional but a document of true conditions in a cotton mill in Derbyshire. The illustration above shows the hero, Michael, ragged and half-starved, embraced by a well-to-do former playmate who has come to look over the factory with a group of rich visitors.

per's ability to convey the finer nuances of his art. The trade was in turmoil. As entrepreneurs flooded the market with single engravings and books of views, old-line publishers had to cut prices to compete, sometimes at fatal cost.

Turner's first blow came in 1839, when publication of his most celebrated folio of engraved reproductions, *Picturesque Views in England and Wales*, abruptly ceased. In 1842 a second publisher who owned the plates based on two well-known Turner paintings, *Ancient Italy* and *Modern Italy*, sold them to a society called the National Art Union, which—thanks to another technological advance, the electrogalvanic process of reproduction—was able to offer impressions to society members at a mere guinea apiece. The same year calamity struck again when another of Turner's publishers went bankrupt. The artist's utter dejection was expressed in a letter to the daughter of his old friend W. F. Wells. "Woe is me," he wrote Clara, "one failure after another is quite enough to make one sick of the whole concern."

The glutting of the engraving market posed another dilemma: people were growing bored with landscapes. Turner had a jolting experience that must have brought back his days as an unknown. To offset his loss of income from reproductions, he decided to seek orders for watercolors, based on new material he had gathered on a sketching tour of Switzerland in 1841. In the past he would have gone ahead on his own, certain of eager buyers. Now he relied on an agent, a respected figure in the art world named Thomas Griffith, to whom he agreed to pay a 10 per cent commission. At the price of 80 guineas per watercolor—less than Turner thought they were worth—Griffith was able to obtain orders for only five of ten proffered works.

Public tastes were turning elsewhere, to pictures of the sentimental and familiar: portraits of prettified young ladies and faithful pets, moralizing anecdotes of home and hearth, literary themes based not on the classics but on popular novels. A new type of art fancier was emerging. He was of the middle class, and, unlike the old-time connoisseur, he was schooled in neither the history nor the esthetics of art. The grand manner of painting, as well as Turner's flights of imagination, put him off; he was more at ease with homelier themes. Where the earlier collector had prided himself on the individuality of his choices, the new devotee was satisfied to share his tastes en masse. Very often he joined an "art union," like the one that sold prints of Turner's works at a guinea apiece. Such societies offered members not only low-priced reproductions but a yearly chance at a raffle for an original oil. This novelty was enough to curdle a connoisseur's blood, but it was wholly in tune with the zest for self-improvement that bloomed with the Victorian age.

In large part Victoria herself shaped the new course of English art. Its theme of sweet—often syrupy—domesticity was one she favored not only in paintings but also in her personal life. With her marriage in 1840 to her handsome cousin, Prince Albert of Saxe-Coburg, she exchanged the scintillating influence of Lord Melbourne for the settling influence of her madly adored husband. The Prince Consort was earnest and high-minded. The couple's early rising after their wedding night

This squat velvet armchair epitomizes both the ornate style and unabashed sentiment of the Victorian era. The carved-walnut grapevines on the back encircle a porcelain plaque copied from Prince Albert's wedding portrait, which is surmounted by the traditional British lion.

raised eyebrows among their courtiers; one, Charles Greville, confided to his diary that it was no way to provide the nation with a Prince of Wales. He was wrong. The first of nine royal offspring, a daughter, was born just nine months later, and in a year was followed by an heir to the throne, the prince who was to become Edward VII.

The English suddenly awoke to the fact that the royal licentiousness of the Georgian era was over. Those of the middle class were especially pleased; they saw an extension of themselves in the solid virtues at the palace. Victoria and Albert went to bed and rose betimes. During the day they sat at adjoining writing tables and methodically worked on household accounts as well as affairs of state. Evenings they eschewed frivolity for chess or music. The Queen's favorite painter, Landseer, who excelled at animal portraits, initiated the royal couple into a secret of his craft: he taught them how to draw a stag.

Albert may have had some private thoughts on this score. As a princely tourist in his premarital days, he had had a good grounding in art, including a talk with the Pope about the works of the Etruscans; his own taste ran to the Italian primitives and to the Flemish. His wife did not know much about art, but she knew what she liked: whatever mirrored the bliss of her family life. Anything beyond this escaped her. After viewing the drawings at Windsor collected by her late uncle George IV—many of them during his bawdy years as Regent—she recorded the fact in the journal she kept. Some of the drawings were arranged so that she could not see them; as she wrote primly, "they were not quite eligible, and were tacked together."

A faintly censorious note was also creeping into officialdom's view of art. The men who governed England wanted to channel artistic efforts to "useful" ends; did not the nation, they asked, owe its very wealth to its practicality? Actually, the belief that art should be harnessed for utilitarian ends predated Victoria. In 1836 a Parliamentary committee had inquired into ways of using the nation's store of artistic talent to improve the look of English manufactures. It spent much time airing the suspicion that the Royal Academy was a cabal to prevent the spread of that talent, and ended by urging a separate Government School of Design —a recommendation promptly adopted by Parliament.

In 1841 the lawmakers stepped in again. A new Palace of Westminster was rising to replace the old quarters of the burned-out Houses of Parliament, and elaborate interior decoration was deemed necessary for such chambers as the Peers' Refreshment Room. Under a Royal Commission headed by the the 22-year-old Prince Albert, a competition was launched for artist-candidates. The decoration decided on was a series of huge wall paintings of scenes from English history and from the works of three native literary titans, Spenser, Shakespeare and Milton. The medium chosen—fresco—was popular in Albert's Germany but almost totally untried in England. The results showed it. By the time the project ended two decades later, most of the frescoes, improperly prepared, had discolored, blistered or mildewed. As one critic put it, the next generation might well wonder if there would have been "less discredit to the national taste" in walls left entirely bare.

In the contest for the fresco commissions Turner played no part. His failure to enter the lists was in some ways surprising. The urge to compete was instinctive to him, and he also still hankered for royal attention; in 1840, en route home from Venice through Germany, he had gone out of his way to Rosenau, the Prince Consort's birthplace, to sketch its castle. On the other hand, work on the frescoes, some of which measured up to 200 square feet, involved an effort more suited to brawny youth, and the proposed style, grandiose and studied, was far from his current predilection.

A kind of special ferocity stamped Turner's art in these early years of the 1840s. It was as if he was aware that time was running out, and was all the more avid to proclaim his artistic beliefs. In quantity alone, his output was remarkable; in addition to the paintings that, unseen, packed his studio, he showed eight at the Academy in 1840, another eight in 1841 and five in 1842. Some were rather trite in treatment as well as in theme, but the general level was high. Among his entries were several superbly expressive views of Venice and three of his most memorable seascapes, their differences proof of Turner's continuing virtuosity.

Prince Albert himself designed this elaborate gilt centerpiece especially for the Queen in 1849. The base is decorated with four of Victoria's favorite dogs—hounds and terriers —along with a dead hare and the rats that the dogs usually hunted. Albert's taste in such things was widely admired and imitated.

One of the latter, *Slavers throwing overboard the dead and dying*, recreated an incident that had occurred before England's recent abolition of its colonial slave trade; a cargo of epidemic-smitten blacks had been dumped because insurance could be collected only on those "lost" at sea and not on those felled by disease. Turner fused the anguish of the victims and the churning of the waters into an epic of horror made even more vivid by colors run wild. A second seascape, *Peace: burial at sea*, recorded the death of Turner's Scottish colleague, Wilkie, while on his way home from Egypt aboard the steamer *Orient*. It is a study in grief, in which black sails and smoke cast a heavy pall on a calm ocean. The third, *Snowstorm*, is the record of Turner's experience in the teeth of a gale on the deck of the steamboat *Ariel*. Despite their differing moods, there is something common to these paintings. Each stems from an actual event, yet in all three, Turner's effect is less anecdotal than symbolic—an intensely subjective statement on man's inexorable rout by the higher power that surrounds him.

Contemporary viewers did not see it this way. Many were irritated by what they regarded as crudities of execution, excesses of color and unseemly revelations of the painter's psyche. Very likely they were also simply tired of Turner; he had been around for an eternity. As a result of the critical response he plummeted from the peak of acclaim he had achieved with *Temeraire*. An occasional compliment came his way out of kindness for an aged artist, and sometimes there was a bit of gentle joshing, as when the irrepressible weekly *Punch* proposed an all-purpose title for a Turner painting: *A Typhoon bursting in a Simoom over the Whirlpool of Maelstrom, Norway; with a ship on fire, an eclipse, and the effect of a lunar rainbow*. But the general reaction to Turner's late works was less benign. It was expressed by a reviewer who summed up several of them as the products of "a diseased eye and a reckless hand."

What the critics and the public favored now was defined by the hit of the Academy exhibition of 1843, a painting called *Solomon Eagle Exhorting the People to Repentance during the Plague of London*. It shows a local prophet-fanatic of the 17th Century invoking judgment on the doomed city and its masked revelers; his classically perfect body is naked except for a loincloth, and a pan of burning charcoal is implausibly balanced on his head. The picture is busy, glossy and adequately but not jarringly melodramatic—everything, in short, that gallery-goers of the time had begun to love. It also shows the distance that separated Turner from the new mainstream of English art.

And yet his career was by no means over, thanks to a battle waged on his behalf by a young man who was to emerge as one of the most singular figures England ever produced: John Ruskin. In time, Ruskin—writer, critic, sometime painter and ultimately sage—would embark on a long reign as supreme arbiter of English art, his word law and his power to make or break unlimited. "The little despot imagines himself the Pope of Art," an embittered painter once said of him, and it was a charge Ruskin would not have denied. Along with acute esthetic perceptions, an eloquent and prolific pen and strong likes and dislikes, he had total faith in his own infallibility. "Until people are ready to receive all I say about art as unquestionable," he wrote, "I don't consider myself to have any reputation at all worth caring about."

It was through his advocacy of Turner that Ruskin commenced his rise. They met in 1840, when Turner was 65 and Ruskin all of 21. This was not their first contact, however. At 16, Ruskin had framed a reply to a fusillade in *Blackwood's Magazine* in which the reviewer demolished a Turner work and declared that "artists are, like cucumbers in a hotbed, forced, and no wonder they run more to belly than to head." Evidently the "black anger" Ruskin later recalled he felt showed in his letter, and his father suggested it be sent to Turner for his prior approval, via an intermediary. Since it was signed simply "J.R. Esq.," Turner was aware of neither the writer's identity nor his age. He wrote back declining the defense with thanks, and revealing an immunity to the fourth estate: "I never move in these matters—they are of no import save mischief."

Ruskin's boyish assumption that he was competent to champion Turner was not as cheeky as it may seem. He was almost insufferably precocious, the only child of a rich sherry merchant and the apple of his eye. In the Ruskins' comfortable villa in suburban London, the pursuit of culture was deemed mandatory. At seven the son of the house had already acquired enough of his unique blend of piety and esthetics to pray that the frost would not spoil the blossoms on the almond trees; his mother planned for him to become a bishop. His true calling beckoned when, at 13, he was given a gift of Samuel Rogers' *Italy*, illustrated by Turner's views. It was love at first sight, followed by the start of a large family collection of original Turner drawings. The young Ruskin reverently placed one in what he termed his "idol niche," and took another with him to Oxford.

He was still an undergraduate when he met his hero at dinner at the home of Turner's agent, Thomas Griffith, who also had dealings with

Ruskin's father. Turner, another guest recalled, took no special notice of Ruskin, but Ruskin was all eyes and ears. Late that night he poured his impressions into his diary. Although Turner had been described to him as "coarse, boorish, unintellectual, vulgar," he found him to be "a somewhat eccentric, keen-mannered, matter-of-fact, English-minded gentleman: good-natured evidently, bad-tempered evidently . . . shrewd, perhaps a little selfish, highly intellectual, the powers of his mind not brought out with any delight in their manifestation, or intention of display, but flashing out occasionally in a word or a look." Almost half a century later Ruskin re-read this passage and proudly noted that it had been "pretty close."

In 1842, enraged by another critical attack on Turner, he started to prepare a pamphlet in reply; it soon evolved into a more ambitious plan for a book. Thus was born what was to burgeon into the most stupendous feat of art commentary in the English language, the five volumes known as *Modern Painters*. The actual title of the first volume was much longer, and merits repeating as an indication of Ruskin's scope and self-assurance—*Modern Painters: their superiority in the art of landscape painting to all The Ancient Masters proved by examples of The True, the Beautiful, and the Intellectual, from the works of modern artists, especially from those of J. M. W. Turner, Esq., R.A.*

Lest his youth draw fire, Ruskin cloaked his identity in the byline "A Graduate of Oxford." The first publisher he went to rejected the book because the public "cared little about Turner." The next publisher proved more receptive, and the book appeared in May of 1843. It caused a sensation; readers could not fail to be dazed, for example, by the fervent assertion that Turner had been "sent as a prophet of God to reveal to men the mysteries of His universe." A second edition was soon required.

Turner himself waited more than a year to thank Ruskin, and then did it with his usual gruffness. Ruskin did not mind; by then they were friends. He often dropped by Turner's gallery, and Turner went to the Ruskins' house on Denmark Hill for the young man's birthday dinners. Turner's attitude toward his brash apologist changed from amused to avuncular. He shared the senior Ruskins' concern about their son's first trip to the Continent "alone" (at 26, and with a valet), and he shared their joy when, at 29, Ruskin married his lively cousin Euphemia Gray—a union fated to be dissolved on the grounds of his impotence.

This portrait of the Egyptian Pacha Muhemed Ali was painted by Romantic artist David Wilkie, Turner's friend and a fellow Academician, who went to the Near East in 1840 to visit and sketch the locales of the Bible. Sailing home, Wilkie died suddenly and was buried at sea. Turner memorialized the event in a poignant seascape. When a colleague criticized it for the blackness of the sails in the picture, Turner replied, "I only wish I had any color to make them blacker."

As well as new friends, Turner gained substantial financial benefit from Ruskin's entry into his life. *Modern Painters* revived the demand for his works; new collectors appeared, and he was able to dispose of a number of paintings passed up by previous buyers. He also made his first American sale—of *Staffa, Fingal's Cave*—to the wealthy James Lenox of New York. At first Turner shied from the transaction, saying that Americans would not "come up to the scratch." Lenox proved him wrong by paying £500, although he admitted to finding *Staffa* "indistinct." Turner's reply to the mutual friend who reported this was: "Tell him that indistinctness is my forte."

Buoyed by the renewed interest in his work, Turner in 1844 pro-

duced what was to be his last masterpiece, and perhaps his greatest: *Rain, Steam, and Speed (pages 158-159)*. An onrushing train crosses a Thames bridge in a downpour—that is the sum of the scene, handled with all the indistinctness of which Turner boasted, and yet with totally convincing visual effect. It is also handled inventively. Turner's first coup was to concentrate on the train—a contrivance that many English still thought of as the devil's handiwork, let alone a fit subject for art. His second coup was to arrange the composition so that the train seems about to hurtle off the canvas; this device for relating the picture to the space beyond the frame, and thus directly involving the viewer, was to become a cardinal tenet of modern painting.

Turner's title for the work also bespeaks a significant change of approach. The steam and speed are man's doing, by way of the locomotive he has devised; only the rain is nature's. Moreover, it is one of nature's less fearsome phenomena. The English are wholly at home with it, unlike the typhoons and avalanches that formerly preoccupied Turner. *Rain, Steam, and Speed* evokes not awe but familiarity. Turner was not a sermonizer, but he may have been making a philosophical point, and for him an unusually hopeful one: that as man extended his own power, he could co-exist more equably with the power of nature.

It was part of Turner's genius that even as he neared 70 he could relish and adapt to his art the advances apparent all around him—advances that heralded fundamental changes in English life. By 1843, the year before *Rain, Steam, and Speed* was exhibited at the Academy, there were already 2,000 miles of railway track throughout the land; in five years there would be 3,000 more. An electric telegraph linked major cities, and soon England's prized insularity would be challenged by the laying of a cable under the Channel to France.

Long-sought legislation to improve the lot of the lower classes was also at hand, under the deft guidance of Sir Robert Peel, Lord Melbourne's successor as Prime Minister. It was Peel who, in an earlier Cabinet role, had given London a new taste of law and order by setting up a metropolitan police force—whose members are still called "bobbies" in his honor. As leader of the government, Peel preferred the label of Conservative to that of Tory; in an augury of the schisms of modern politics, his Whig opponents adopted the countering label of Liberals.

Under Peel's ministry the hated Corn Laws, which had long protected big landowners and plagued the poor with high food prices, were at last wiped off the books, and measures were enacted to ease the working conditions of women and children. Women were barred from mine work, and limited to a 12-hour day in factories; children under 13 were no longer permitted to work at night. The vested interests vilified Peel as a traitor to his kind. But history has judged him a benefactor of the propertied classes because he taught them not to fight progress, but to yield to it.

Around 1845, Turner's health began to go. Only the year before he had felt strong enough for a sketching tour of the Alps and Rhine valleys, tramping so tirelessly that in mid-journey he had had to have his boots retapped. This year he made another tour, but only as far as the Channel coast of France. It was his last foray abroad. From now on he

When the first world's fair, the Great Exhibition, opened in London on May 1, 1851, half the floor space in the celebrated Crystal Palace was occupied by British goods. The gamut of English inventiveness ran from displays of heavy machinery *(above)* to a "Medieval Court" *(below)*, featuring pseudo-Gothic church furnishings made in England. Moved by the splendor of the show on opening day, Victoria wrote in her journal: "God bless my dearest country, which has shown itself so great today."

spent more and more time with the comforts offered by Chelsea and Sophia Booth, and less and less time in London. The house on Queen Anne Street became increasingly run down until it looked, as a friend put it, like "a place . . . where the tax gatherer had long ceased to call, which no one would inhabit, and about which the landlord himself had abandoned all hope."

Turner, too, suffered infirmities. Among other ills of old age, he had to cope with the loss of his teeth; he would not use the false set that was made for him, and he took in very little food. Drink proved an all-too-welcome substitute. The local "surgeon dentist and cupper" who attended him reported that he consumed "sometimes two quarts of milk per day and rum in proportion, very frequently to excess."

Ruskin later asserted that Turner's physical decline was matched by a loss of mental powers, so that his mind was actually "clouded." The evidence disputes this. For a time, when the Academy's president fell sick, Turner served as deputy, and filled the post well. When asked, he still offered excellent advice to respectful juniors, sometimes just grunting a word of opinion, sometimes making his point right on the canvas with a brush. (One minor painter so favored was offered 300 guineas for his canvas because the great man had daubed at it.)

Indeed, Turner continued exhibiting right through 1850, the year before he died. That his paintings became more cryptic and gloomy is not altogether surprising in an introvert awaiting the end. His letters, however, were cheerful enough. One correspondent was Hawksworth Fawkes, son of his old patron, who devotedly supplied Turner at Christmastime with a goose or a brace of hares. Genially acknowledging these gifts that he could not enjoy, Turner sounded lively and alert. With typical enthusiasm he wrote of a new marvel of iron and glass that was rising on the London scene—the Crystal Palace, built to house the Great Exhibition of 1851 that stunned millions of visitors with the exploits of the new technology.

In December of 1851 Turner failed perceptibly. A doctor who was summoned to his bedroom at Chelsea told him he was dying. Turner wryly suggested the doctor go downstairs, have a glass of sherry and then take another look. The judgment stood. Early on the 19th, the winter sun broke through an overcast sky, and Turner asked to be moved so that he could see it. The keen gray eyes that had so long been accustomed, as one admirer put it, "to looking straight at the face of nature through fair and foul weather alike" wanted one last sight of it.

Within the hour Turner was dead. The cause was certified to be "natural decay." His body was taken to the Queen Anne Street house and put on view in the gallery. On the 30th, a cortege that included many of his fellow Academicians bore the coffin to St. Paul's Cathedral. Choristers sang the Death March from Handel's oratorio *Saul*, the final service was said and Turner was placed in the crypt, as he had wished, beside the tombs of Sir Joshua Reynolds and Sir Thomas Lawrence.

That afternoon Turner's executors went back to Queen Anne Street for the reading of the will. If they also read the London *Times*, they knew by then that they were in for trouble. On December 23rd an obit-

The international sections of the fair offered products from exotic lands. When China refused to submit anything, English importers assembled an exhibit *(above)* from their stores and even provided a Chinese to act as host. From India came a howdah that was displayed on a stuffed elephant *(below)* borrowed from a local museum. The profusion of exhibits led the novelist Charles Dickens to lament: "There's too much. I have a natural horror of sights, and the fusion of so many sights in one has not decreased it."

uary had noted that "Mr. Turner undoubtedly realized a very large fortune . . . he was not known to have any relations." On the 24th a letter to the editor begged to differ. Its point was terse: "Mr. Turner had five first cousins at his decease; one of them is my mother." The writer was one Jabez Tepper, who happened, conveniently, to be a lawyer. Thus was fired the opening gun in a long, tortuous and successful battle to frustrate Turner's design for disposing of his money and his art.

Among the few bequests that escaped unscathed in the ensuing litigation was a £150 annuity for Sophia and a sum just sixpence short of £20 for Ruskin, for the express purpose of buying a mourning ring, a Victorian custom among friends. Commenting on the amount—fixed to avoid a tax on legacies of £20 or more—Ruskin senior told his son: "Nobody can say you were paid to praise." Other minor bequests Turner made out of apparent anxiety lest he be forgotten—such as a sum to the Academy for a gold or silver medal for landscape painting "with my name upon it"—had to await the pleasure of his relatives.

What they were after was a fortune conservatively estimated at £140,000. Most of it was in real estate and in stocks; a telling footnote on Turner's habits was provided when his household effects were valued at only £102, and his wardrobe inventoried at six pairs of trousers, two waistcoats and three cravats. In years of adding and canceling codicils to his will, Turner had never swerved in the purpose for which he intended the bulk of his fortune: the establishment of a home, on land he owned near London, for "Poor and Decayed Male Artists born in England and of English Parents only and lawful issue."

His relatives were defeated in an attempt to prevent probate on the ground that Turner was of unsound mind, but they pressed on in the courts and in 1856 found the flaw they sought. By English law, land for charitable purposes could not be bequeathed by a will alone; Turner, aware of this, had had a deed prepared conveying the land to his trustees, but by what seems an incredible oversight he had neglected to send them the documents as required by law. Seizing upon this loose end, his relatives managed to unravel a large part of the will. In the end, the five cousins whom Turner had rarely if ever seen, and to whom he had left nothing, divided his money among themselves.

The second major provision of the will concerned Turner's art. He bequeathed his "finished pictures" to the National Gallery, on condition that it add a "room or rooms" to house them, to be called Turner's Gallery. If this were not done within 10 years after his death, the paintings were to remain at Queen Anne Street, there to be exhibited, free, to the public. Wherever they ended up, Turner's clear intent for his pictures was to keep them together, away from the distraction of other painters' works, as an entity that would trace the scope of his art.

The problem before the National Gallery was gigantic and complex. One difficulty was the state of many of Turner's works. Through a cracked skylight in his gallery, the elements he loved had intruded to spot, flake and mildew many canvases; Ruskin's father, viewing the wreckage after the place had been aired and dusted, was reminded of the excavations at Pompeii. Another and far more vexing matter was the need to decide which pictures were "finished" and which were not. The riddle haunts scholars to this day; some of Turner's currently most admired oils, such as *Norham Castle (pages 160-161)*, may have been merely preparatory "lay-ins" on which he expected to work further. Unwittingly, Turner's relatives helped the National Gallery to avoid the decision. Although they had won the Queen Anne Street house itself, they were either indifferent to its treasures or ignorant of their value. The Gallery got not only the "finished" oils Turner had left it, but all the "unfinished" oils and the drawings as well.

For years the Turner Bequest weighed on the Gallery like an incubus. Some officials frankly disdained its worth. Those who did not still had the headache of finding space for some 300 oils, not to mention the 300 watercolors and 19,000 drawings. Most of this hoard was consigned to storerooms as "lumber," except for about 100 oils that were deemed finished. Two months before the end of the 10-year time limit Turner had imposed, these oils, plus a few watercolors, were jammed into two regular exhibition rooms set off by placards with the words "Turner's Gallery" written on them.

The issue nagged on, with questions asked in Parliament but unresolved. Meanwhile, Thornbury's biography spread the impression of Turner as a reprobate, and in the ensuing stir few heard of a letter sent in 1877 to a London art dealer by a group of young French artists. They described themselves as having struggled "for ten years against convention and routine . . . applying . . . with passion to the rendering of reality of form in movement as well as to the fugitive phenomena of light." They could not forget, they said, that they had been "preceded in this path by a great master of the English School, the illustrious Turner." Among those signing the tribute were Degas, Monet, Pissarro and Renoir.

In time the Turner Bequest began to be dispersed. By Parliamentary act some paintings were sent to provincial museums, and others later to museums abroad. Officials argued that in this way they would be more accessible to more viewers. And so Turner was defeated in his dream of keeping his works together. But time brought some recompense. In 1905 his "unfinished" efforts began to be removed from their hiding place, and young 20th Century painters could begin to take the full measure of his uniquely prophetic art.

Ruskin once wrote that when Turner died there would be "more of nature and her mysteries forgotten in one sob than will be learned again by the eyes of a generation." Behind the passion of this prediction lay a truth that Ruskin could not have foreseen. We do not look at nature today as it was looked at in Turner's time. Jet travel at 30,000 feet precludes the loving scrutiny of a single tree, and other wonders clamor for attention: the view of a plant under a powerful microscope, the televised sight of outer space through an astronaut's window. It is a world that 19th Century landscape painters would have neither understood nor liked—with the probable exception of Turner. Free expression was his faith; imagination his great gift. Surely he would have enjoyed a try at the landscape of the moon.

A Lifelong Journey

In addition to his public output of art, Turner painted almost 20,000 private, experimental watercolors. Discovered in his sketchbooks, they constitute a personal diary, not only of his many trips through England and the Continent but also of the artistic journey he made away from the conventions of his time toward the timelessness of abstraction. Turner began this exploration as a topographical watercolorist; he made line drawings of specific places, shaded them with washes and tints, then colored in the details, even the feathers of barnyard chickens *(opposite)*. As a young man, he painted a section of old London Bridge realistically *(page 178)*, and by making it almost fill the page, he emphasized its monumentality. As the following pages show, however, he was moving toward an art concerned less with form and more with color. On his first trip to Italy in 1819 he saw the radiant colors revealed by southern light. Color later enthralled him so completely that in a French river scene the drawn lines all but vanish under strokes of red-orange, blue and yellow-green; a view of Venice dissolves in slashes of pink, green and white on brown paper. No line appears at all in a watercolor that captures the fury of an Italian storm; a drawing of building façades is as two-dimensional as the abstract band of yellow wash beneath it. Finally, in a page from a sketchbook called "Color Beginnings" *(page 184)*, Turner transforms some of nature's hues into those of art alone.

The young Turner's watercolor palette contained the same colors that dominated his oil paintings: traditional, academic, earth browns and greys. He even used them to dull down the yellow of sunlight pouring over the gateway of an English manor house in the striking, but conventional, watercolor at the right, which he painted at the age of 23.

Manor House Gateway, 1798

Old London Bridge, 1796-1797

St. Peter's from the South, 1819

Honfleur, 1826-1833

Venice, buildings, 1839

Paestum in Storm, after 1830

. . . Turner differs from all other men whose work I have studied. He never draws accurately on the spot, with the intention of modifying or composing afterwards from the materials; but instantly modifies as he draws, placing his memoranda where they are to be ultimately used, and taking exactly what he wants, not a fragment or line more.

He never throughout his life was pleased with things that stood quite straight up. . . . Usually he sets all his cathedral and church towers from three to six feet off the perpendicular, being provoked with them for not behaving gracefully, like ships in a breeze.

It is first to be remembered that in every one of his English or French drawings, Turner's mind was, in two great instincts, at variance with itself. The affections of it clung . . . to humble scenery, and gentle wildness of pastoral life. But the admiration of it was, more than any other artist's whatsoever, fastened on largeness of scale. . . . Hence . . . he was continually endeavoring to reconcile old fondnesses with new sublimities.

Turner's merit. . .consists in this, that, from his tenth year to his seventieth, he never passed a day, and seldom an hour, without obtaining the accurate knowledge of some great natural fact; and, never forgetting anything he once knew, he keeps expressing this enormous and accumulated knowledge.

John Ruskin

Chronology: Artists of Turner's Era

1700   1800   1900   1700   1800   1900

ENGLAND
WILLIAM HOGARTH 1697-1764
ALLAN RAMSAY (Scottish) 1713-1784
RICHARD WILSON 1714-1782
ALEXANDER COZENS c.1717-1786
SIR JOSHUA REYNOLDS 1723-1792
GAVIN HAMILTON (Scottish) 1723-1798
GEORGE STUBBS 1724-1806
PAUL SANDBY 1725-1809
THOMAS GAINSBOROUGH 1727-1788
JOHANN ZOFFANY (German) 1733-1810
GEORGE ROMNEY 1734-1802
ANGELICA KAUFFMAN (Swiss) 1741-1807
JOHN HENRY FUSELI (Swiss) 1741-1825
JOHN ROBERT COZENS 1752-c.1797/9
THOMAS ROWLANDSON 1756-1827
WILLIAM BLAKE 1757-1827
JOHN HOPPNER 1759-1810
GEORGE MORLAND 1763-1804
JOHN CROME 1768-1821
SIR THOMAS LAWRENCE 1769-1830
THOMAS GIRTIN 1775-1802
JOSEPH MALLORD WILLIAM TURNER 1775-1851
JOHN CONSTABLE 1776-1837
CORNELIUS VARLEY 1781-1873
JOHN SELL COTMAN 1782-1842
DAVID COX 1783-1859
SIR DAVID WILKIE 1785-1841
BENJAMIN ROBERT HAYDON 1786-1846
WILLIAM ETTY 1787-1849
JOHN MARTIN 1789-1854
RICHARD PARKES BONINGTON 1802-1828
SIR EDWIN LANDSEER 1802-1873
SAMUEL PALMER 1805-1881
ALFRED STEVENS 1817-1875
FORD MADOX BROWN 1821-1893
WILLIAM HOLMAN HUNT 1827-1910
DANTE GABRIEL ROSSETTI 1828-1882
SIR JOHN EVERETT MILLAIS 1829-1896
SIR EDWARD BURNE-JONES 1833-1898
ALPHONSE LEGROS 1837-1911
ALFRED SISLEY 1839-1899

GERMANY
ANTON RAPHAEL MENGS 1728-1779
JUAN ANDRÉS MERCKLEIN ?-1797
CASPAR DAVID FRIEDRICH 1774-1840

FRANCE
JEAN-MARC NATTIER 1685-1766
JEAN-BAPTISTE-SIMÉON CHARDIN 1699-1779
FRANÇOIS BOUCHER 1703-1770
MAURICE-QUENTIN DE LA TOUR 1704-1788
CLAUDE-JOSEPH VERNET 1714-1789
JEAN-BAPTISTE GREUZE 1725-1805
FRANÇOIS-HUBERT DROUAIS 1727-1775
JEAN-HONORÉ FRAGONARD 1732-1806
JACQUES-LOUIS DAVID 1748-1825
LOUISE ELISABETH VIGÉE-LEBRUN 1755-1842
PIERRE PRUD'HON 1758-1823
GEORGES MICHEL 1763-1843
JEAN-AUGUSTE-DOMINIQUE INGRES 1780-1867
THÉODORE GÉRICAULT 1791-1824
CAMILLE COROT 1796-1875
EUGÈNE DELACROIX 1798-1863
CONSTANTIN GUYS 1802-1892
HONORÉ DAUMIER 1808-1879
THÉODORE ROUSSEAU 1812-1867
JEAN-FRANÇOIS MILLET 1814-1875
GUSTAVE COURBET 1819-1877
EUGÈNE BOUDIN 1824-1898
PIERRE PUVIS DE CHAVANNES 1824-1898
ÉDOUARD MANET 1832-1883
EDGAR DEGAS 1834-1917

SPAIN
FRANCISCO GOYA 1746-1828

UNITED STATES
JOHN SINGLETON COPLEY 1737-1815
BENJAMIN WEST 1738-1820
WASHINGTON ALLSTON 1779-1843
THOMAS SULLY 1783-1872
JOHN JAMES AUDUBON 1785-1851
SAMUEL F. B. MORSE 1791-1872
GEORGE CATLIN 1796-1872
THOMAS COLE 1801-1848
JOHN QUIDOR 1801-1881
WILLIAM SIDNEY MOUNT 1807-1868
GEORGE CALEB BINGHAM 1811-1879
DAVID GILMOUR BLYTHE 1815-1865
GEORGE INNESS 1825-1894
FREDERIC EDWIN CHURCH 1826-1900
JAMES ABBOTT MCNEILL WHISTLER 1834-1903
WINSLOW HOMER 1836-1910

1700   1800   1900   1700   1800   1900

Turner's predecessors, contemporaries and successors are grouped chronologically by country. The bands correspond to the artists' lifespans.

Bibliography

*Available in Paperback

TURNER—HIS LIFE AND WORKS

Burnet, John, *Turner and His Works*. David Bogue, London, 1852.
Butlin, Martin, *The Later Works of J.M.W. Turner*.* Tate Gallery, London. Published by Order of the Trustees, 1965.
——, *Turner Watercolors*. Watson-Guptill Publications, 1965.
——, *Watercolours from the Turner Bequest 1819-1845*. Tate Gallery, London, 1962.
Chamot, Mary, *The Early Works of J.M.W. Turner*.* Tate Gallery, London. Published by Order of the Trustees, 1965.
Falk, Bernard, *Turner the Painter: His Hidden Life*. Hutchinson & Co., Ltd., London, 1938.
Finberg, A. J., *The Life of J.M.W. Turner, R.A.* (revised edition). Oxford at the Clarendon Press, 1962.
——(editor), *A Complete Inventory of the Drawings of the Turner Bequest*, 2 vols. By Order of the Trustees. Darling & Son, Ltd., London, 1909.
——, *Turner's Sketches & Drawings*.* Introduction by Lawrence Gowing. Schocken Books, 1968.
Gowing, Lawrence, *Turner: Imagination and Reality* (exhibition catalogue).* The Museum of Modern Art, 1966.
Herrmann, Luke, *Ruskin and Turner*. Faber & Faber, London, 1968.
Kitson, Michael, *Turner*.* Barnes & Noble, Inc., 1965.
Lindsay, Jack, *J.M.W. Turner: His Life and Work, A Critical Biography*. New York Graphic Society, 1966.
——(editor), *The Sunset Ship: The Poems of J.M.W. Turner*. Scorpion Press, 1966.
Rothenstein, John and Martin Butlin, *Turner*. George Braziller, 1964.
Thornbury, Walter, *The Life of J.M.W. Turner, R.A.* (revised edition). Chatto & Windus, Piccadilly, London, 1877.

CONSTABLE—HIS LIFE AND WORKS

Baskett, John, *Constable Oil Sketches*. Watson-Guptill Publications, 1966.
Beckett, R. B. (editor), *The Complete Correspondence of John Constable*, Vols. 1-5. The Suffolk Records Society, London.
Leslie, C. R., *Memoirs of the Life of John Constable*. Composed chiefly of his letters. The Phaidon Press, London, 1951.
Peacock, Carlos, *John Constable: The Man and His Work*. New York Graphic Society, 1965.
Pool, Phoebe, *John Constable*.* Barnes & Noble, Inc., 1964.
Reynolds, Graham, *Constable, the Natural Painter*. McGraw-Hill Book Company, 1965.

ART-HISTORICAL BACKGROUND

Bell, Quentin, *Victorian Artists*. Routledge & Kegan Paul, Ltd., London, 1967.
Boase, T.S.R., *English Art 1800-1870*. The Oxford History of English Art, Vol. X. Oxford at the Clarendon Press, 1959.
Clark, Kenneth, *Landscape into Art*.* Beacon Press, 1961.

Gaunt, William, *A Concise History of English Painting*.* Praeger World of Art Series. Frederick A. Praeger, Publishers, 1964.
Hill, Draper, *Mr. Gillray, the Caricaturist*. The Phaidon Press, London, 1965.
Newton, Eric, *The Romantic Rebellion*.* Schocken Books, 1964.
Painting in England 1700-1850 (exhibition catalogue, 2 vols., text and plates).* Collection of Mr. and Mrs. Paul Mellon. Virginia Museum of Fine Arts, 1963.
Romantic Art in Britain: Paintings and Drawings 1760-1860 (exhibition catalogue).* Detroit Institute of Art, Philadelphia Museum of Art, 1968.
Rosenblum, Robert, *Transformations in Late Eighteenth Century Art*. Princeton University Press, 1967.
Ruskin, John, *Modern Painters*, 5 vols. Dana Estes & Company.
Waterhouse, Ellis, *Painting in Britain 1530-1790*. The Pelican History of Art Series. Penguin Books, 1953.
Wilenski, R. H., *English Painting*. Hale, Cushman and Flint, 1937.

CULTURAL AND HISTORICAL BACKGROUND

Burton, Elizabeth, *The Pageant of Georgian England*. Charles Scribner's Sons, 1967.
Fisher, H.A.L., *Napoleon*. Oxford University Press, 1952.
Fulford, Roger, *George the Fourth*. Duckworth, London, 1935.
Gershoy, Leo, *The French Revolution and Napoleon*. Appleton-Century-Crofts, 1964.
Gordon, George (Lord Byron), "Childe Harold's Pilgrimage." From *The Complete Poetical Works of Byron*. Edited by Paul E. More. The Riverside Press, 1933.
Green, John Richard, *A Short History of the English People*, 2 vols. E.P. Dutton & Co., Everyman's Library, 1917.
Houghton, Walter E., *The Victorian Frame of Mind 1830-1870*. Yale University Press, 1957.
Leslie, Anita, *Mrs. Fitzherbert*. Charles Scribner's Sons, 1960.
Leslie, Doris, *The Great Corinthian*. A portrait of the Prince Regent. Eyre & Spottiswoode, London, 1952.
Markham, Felix, M.H., *Napoleon*.* New American Library, Mentor Books.
Plumb, J. H., *The First Four Georges*. The Macmillan Company, 1957.
Pritchett, V. S., *London Perceived*. Photographs by Evelyn Hofer. Harcourt, Brace & World, Inc., 1962.
Redman, Alvin, *The House of Hanover*. Coward-McCann, 1960.
Richardson, Joanna, *George the IV: A Portrait*. Sidgwick and Jackson, Ltd., London, 1966.
Spar, Francis (general editor), *Le Style Anglais 1750-1850*. Collection Connaissance des Arts. Hachette, Paris, 1959.
Stanley, Arthur (pseu., A. S. Megaw), *Under Italian Skies, An Anthology*. Victor Gollancz Ltd., London, 1950.
Steegman, John, *Consort of Taste, 1830-1870*. Sidgwick and Jackson, Ltd., London, 1950.
Summerson, John, *Georgian London*. Charles Scribner's Sons, 1946.
Trevelyan, G. M., *British History in the Nineteenth Century and After (1782-1919)* (new edition). Longmans, Green and Co., 1937.
——, *Illustrated English Social History*, Vols. 3 and 4. Longmans, Green and Co., 1952.

Picture Credits

The sources for the illustrations in this book appear below. Credits for pictures from left to right are separated by semicolons, from top to bottom by dashes.

SLIPCASE—Frank Lerner

FRONT END PAPERS—Derek Bayes

BACK END PAPERS—Derek Bayes

CHAPTER 1: 6—Graves Art Gallery, Sheffield, by permission of Sheffield Corporation. 17—Graves Art Gallery, Sheffield, courtesy the Guild of Saint George. 19—Metropolitan Museum of Art photo—Museum of Fine Arts, Boston. 21 through 23—Derek Bayes. 24,25—Derek Bayes—Heinz Zinram (2). 26 through 28—Derek Bayes. 29—Worcester Public Library, Worcester, Massachusetts. 30,31—Detroit Institute of Art.
CHAPTER 2: 32—Tate Gallery, London, 34,35—John R. Freeman. 36—Sotheby & Co., London. 38—Collection of Mr. & Mrs. Kurt F. Pantzer, Indianapolis. 40—Detail from *The Lover's Dream*, photo by John R. Freeman. 43—T.S.R. Boase, London. 45 through 51—Derek Bayes.
CHAPTER 3: 52—National Portrait Gallery, London. 56—Detail from *The First Kiss This Ten Years*, by James Gillray, photo by John R. Freeman. 57—Cliché des Musées Nationaux. 59—Time-Life Picture Collection. 61—Victoria & Albert Museum, London. 62—National Portrait Gallery, London. 63—Victoria & Albert Museum, London. 65—Derek Bayes. 66,67—Tate Gallery, London. 68—National Gallery, London. 69 through 75—Derek Bayes.
CHAPTER 4: 76—National Portrait Gallery, London. 78—Photo courtesy American Heritage Publishing Co., Inc. 82—Derek Bayes. 85—Courtesy Wellington Museum, London. 86—Derek Bayes. 88 through 92—Evelyn Hofer. 93 through 97—Derek Bayes. 98,99—Tate Gallery, London. 100 through 102—Derek Bayes. 103 through 107—Evelyn Hofer.
CHAPTER 5: 108,109—Derek Bayes. 110—Courtauld Institute of Art, Copyright Earl of Munster. 112—Royal Pavilion, Brighton (2). 119—National Gallery, London. 120,121—National Gallery, London. 122,123—Derek Bayes. 124, 125—Victoria & Albert Museum, London. 126—Barrie & Rockliff, courtesy Victoria & Albert Museum, London. 127—Derek Bayes. 128,129—Barrie & Rockliff, courtesy Victoria & Albert Museum, London. 130 through 132—Derek Bayes. 133—Victoria & Albert Museum, London. 134,135—Derek Bayes—Victoria & Albert Museum, London (2). 136,137—Victoria & Albert Museum.
CHAPTER 6: 138—Derek Bayes. 140—The Bettmann Archive. 142—Photo courtesy John Herron Art Museum, Indianapolis. 148—Derek Bayes. 149—The Library Company, Philadelphia. 153—Derek Bayes. 154,155—Frank Lerner. 156,157—National Gallery of Art, Washington, D.C. 158,159—National Gallery, London. 160,161—Tate Gallery, London. 162,163—Derek Bayes.
CHAPTER 7: 164—National Gallery, London. 166—From *Art and The Industrial Revolution*, Francis D. Klingender, published by Evelyn Adams & Mackay. 168—From *The Victorian Scene* by Nicolas Bentley, Weidenfeld and Nicolson. 169—Copyright reserved to Her Majesty The Queen. 171—Tate Gallery, London. 172,173—Frank Lerner. 177 through 184—Derek Bayes. 188—National Gallery, London.

Acknowledgments

For their help in the preparation of this book, the author and editors wish to thank the following persons and institutions: British Museum, Print Room, London; Martin Butlin, Keeper, British Collection, Tate Gallery, London; Michael V. Levey, Keeper, National Gallery, London; Marie Montembault, Cabinet des Dessins, Musée du Louvre, Paris; Kurt F. Pantzer, Indianapolis; The National Gallery, London; The Tate Gallery, London; Victoria and Albert Museum, Print Room, London.

The Fighting "Temeraire," 1838

Index

Numerals in italics indicate a picture of the subject mentioned. Unless otherwise identified, all listed art works are by Turner. Dimensions are given in inches unless otherwise noted; height precedes width.

The text for this book was photocomposed in Bodoni Book, a typeface named for its Italian designer, Giambattista Bodoni (1740-1813). One of the earliest modern typefaces, Bodoni Book differs from more evenly weighted old-style characters in the greater contrast between thick and thin parts of letters. The Bodoni character is vertical with a thin, straight serif.

PRINTED IN U.S.A.